C000146003

SHE LIVES LIMITLESSLY

JANE BAKER

CONTENTS

DEDICATION

This book is dedicated to my family; I know cheesy, right?

I'm not usually one of those overly cheesy people, and I promise this isn't the theme of the book, but I can't talk about limitless living without mentioning them.

If someone had told over ten years ago that I'd be sitting here having moved abroad and now writing my own book, I'd have thought they were smoking something crazy, whilst I had dreams, I wasn't in a place where I could ever imagine them happening.

But here I am, having done it and I wouldn't have done any of it without my family. So this book is dedicated to them. To my husband for his unwavering support even when I'm sure my goals seemed crazy, he never once said I couldn't do it and, to this day, has never doubted me. To my children, for the new outlook and lease of life that they gave me, for the privilege of being able to be their mother and watch them grow into amazing little people.

I'm also dedicating this book to every person who's ever felt lost in the world, who's ever been told that they can't or that they'll never amount to anything. I proved them all wrong; I found my place in the world, I made my dreams come true, and I know you can do it too!

Jane xx

Chapter One

INTRODUCTION TO HIGH-END SELLING

When people think of living limitlessly or having freedom in their business, they usually picture the laptop lifestyle with automated funnels and masses of low prices online courses. Still, there's another way, and that other way is high-end selling.

When I first started online in 2013, I also thought that to get the freedom I desired that I didn't have in my first business, I'd need to go down the path of online courses and low-end offerings (spoiler alert it didn't work like that for me!). Still, actually there was another way for me to get the freedom and income I desired, and it didn't involve a single low-end offer.

I leveraged high end selling to supercharge my results;

it's one of the reasons I completely love it. I love high end selling for many reasons, but by far the biggest is the fact that you can legit go from 0 to your dream sales in a really short space of time. I've helped clients go from 0 to replacing their yearly corporate wage in just two weeks, from 0 to 10k in sales in just one week and so much more. If you're looking to supercharge, then high-end selling is the key you've been waiting for!

The benefits of high-end offerings and selling go deeper than just that; it enables you to work less while earning more. For many people, 10k months are the big starting point of their freedom, and depending on where you start with your high-end offers, you could be hitting that with four or less sales each month, just four. The numbers required really aren't all that big when you think there are billions of people in the world, millions of whom could be your ideal client. You only need to get in front of a small number to make the numbers you desire that enable you to start living that life of freedom you've got your eye on.

One thing I don't think people consider when it comes to living that freedom lifestyle using online courses and low-end offerings is that you need a volume of traffic. For many just starting out or looking to really grow, they simply don't have the audience and or budget to drive that volume of traffic they need and so their laptop lifestyle stays a distant dream away. At the same time, they tweak yet another new funnel that not enough people are going to go through.

A question I'm asked regularly about high-end packages and selling is, "Can you get into it even if you're just starting out?" The answer is yes!

This is where supercharging comes in, high-end selling speeds the whole process up and also gives you the information you need at a later date to scale using online courses and automated funnels if that's something you desire.

The other thing that high-end selling enables you to do is gather the information you'll eventually need to build funnels and sell online courses with ease if it's something you've got your eye on scaling into further down the line. You see, aside from volume of traffic, one of the other reasons people struggle with selling online courses and low-end products, to begin with, is because they simply don't know enough or understand the conversion triggers and points of their ideal clients. Hence, they simply aren't able to create offers that sell and or have funnels that convert correctly, meaning they sink all of these hours into creating and tweaking and tinkering with things they'll never get to work for them until they have the information they need.

When you flip it and start with high-end, you don't need to know all of those conversion triggers and points in the same way you do for funnels. You can, in fact, simplify the whole process down and as you'll be mostly selling in a more 1:1 way VS 1:many, you will be able to tailor your pitches and selling conversations to the exact lead VS having to write copy without enough conversion information on your ideal clients to actually write copy that converts en masse.

After making high-end sales, you'll know what converted people; you'll understand what words they used, and what you said in almost all of your conversions that got people across the line and purchasing. You will have real information on what their triggers into purchasing were, and you'll also be able to recognise and see patterns around what people really purchased this for. You can then use all of that information to sell other things, and for online courses and funnels, that information is key.

But what is high-end? Do I need to be selling 50k packages that include champagne dinners?

It's always such a good question, but for me, high-end

selling is whatever you choose to make it. For some people, high-end selling is anything above 2.5k; for others, it's anything above 6k, it really does come down to you and where you might start isn't necessarily where you'll be in twelve months either. When I first started with high-end packages in my coaching business, I thought 3k was a lot, but then twelve months later, I had packages priced 10k and above; these days, I have packages that are 50k and above as well as smaller ones.

I have never been a fan of cookie-cutter approaches, and that's the same for this, what someone else sees as the high-end figure isn't necessarily for you, and that's fine. As a general rule of thumb, I tend to say anything above 6k is high-end, but if you see 2.5k as a high-end starting point for you, then roll with it, there's always room to go up, right?

I think when people think of high-end, they often get distracted and imagine the yachts and champagne dinners and all this glitzy stuff, and for some businesses sure they're awesome things to have in your high-end packages. Still, they're certainly not compulsory, and they don't actually make the package high-end anyway. What makes the package high end is the experience and the result, and unless champagne dinners and yachts are something your ideal clients would deem as valuable, then they really don't serve a purpose inside of your high-end packages.

The other question that often comes along with this is, "I don't live an amazing VIP lifestyle, how will I be able to sell high-end?"

It has nothing to do with that honestly, selling high end isn't about whether you dine at the Eiffel Tower every week it's about the value you bring and the experience you offer your ideal clients.

"But is this something I can actually do with my business?"

The simple answer to this is, yes, 100%. Whether you're a bookkeeper, personal stylist, coach, or nutritionist, high-end selling is possible for you because every single one of you brings value to your client's lives. I've worked with almost every sector I can think of, and they've all been able to sell high-end packages.

I'm always amazed when I say this to people and they will reply with "What even me, I'm an interior designer" and I'm like yes, even you!

It's completely and entirely possible for everyone no matter what business you run high-end selling is possible for you, it's simply about taking what you do and then packaging it in a high-end way, and that's the easy part.

I think in this day and age, particularly if you're in the online space, it's easy to get swept up in the belief that the only people who sell high-end are business coaches or those who offer a financial return, but it's totally not true.

People value so much in their lives, and they value a lot of other things that aren't money, whether we're talking relationships, health and wellness, their time, or even spirituality and religion. We value so much, and so much of what you do probably has a positive effect in various areas of their lives, so are you valuable? Yes.

Are you high-end valuable? Absolutely!

And don't let that fear or belief that might have just popped up in your head right now try to tell you you're not, because you are, trust me on that one for now.

Ultimately high-end selling is for you if you're looking to leverage your time but still really increase your income, whether you're looking to scale your income or maybe you're just getting started, high-end selling is for you. It can unlock so many amazing things not only in your life but for your clients too.

Let's not forget, it isn't all about you; it's about those you serve too, and for them, high-end selling offers them an amazing experience. It enables them to be served at the highest level by you; it allows them to experience something truly valuable and wonderful for themselves, and that is an amazing thing to be able to offer in this world.

"I don't want to be seen as a money grabber."

Selling high-end isn't about that, not unless you're only doing what you do for the money, in which case this book probably isn't for you anyway. Living limitlessly isn't about just making loads of cash; it's about living a life without limits on your terms, and that includes having a business you love whilst doing work you love.

Being seen as a money grabber is definitely a real fear for people, and it's definitely something that I see people attach to high-end selling, the thing is though, who says you would be? Other than someone having a rant in a social media group about a price they've seen someone charge that they don't like.

I personally always think that's more a reflection on their own beliefs than it is on the person charging the prices.

The fact is high-end selling enables you to serve people on

a level that you simply can't achieve through low-end selling, high-end selling also allows you to truly step into your value and own it in this world, and why shouldn't you?

High-end selling isn't for everyone, just like selling mass online courses isn't for everyone either, but there'll always be people who hold beliefs one way or another about people that sell at different price points.

I could very easily find people who hold a belief that people who sell low-end aren't good enough, is it a belief I hold? No.

My point is there's always people out there with beliefs on both sides of the coin no matter what you're discussing; the question always comes down to what beliefs you choose to move forward with in your life.

We shouldn't be afraid to own our value; neither should we be afraid of saying, "I want to serve people at the highest level, and I want to do it in a way that means I'm truly impacting them." It's also not something to be ashamed of if you want to work in a way that keeps the human interaction and engagement, something that high-end selling enables you to do in a way that other levels don't.

The only real answer to this question is, do you feel as if

you'd be doing this just for the money? If the answer hand on your heart is no, then that's all that matters!

Only Americans can sell high-end.

If you're from the USA, you might be reading that and thinking how odd, but it's something that I come across way more times than I'd like to admit.

It's easy to see why as well, generally speaking, most people in the online world will have come across people who sell high-end, and a large percentage of them will be from the USA. It's therefore easy to assume that it's only relevant for that market, but that assumption would be incorrect.

I have high-end clients stretched right out across the globe, all over Europe, the Southern Hemisphere, South America, and India. My clients sell high-end right across the globe too.

You're just as likely to sell a high-end offer in the UK as you are anywhere else, and the online world means you have access to all of that market.

Your location doesn't have any bearing on whether you can sell high-end, you can, and that's the end of that!

Chapter Two

MY STORY

*H*ave you ever had this moment where you're in a room full of people, and yet you feel as if you're all alone?

That was me; I always knew I was destined for more, that I was here to do more, but it took me a few years to figure out what that looked like and to actually do something about it. Life wasn't straightforward for me growing up, but despite this, I always had that feeling of not belonging, of being destined for more. I couldn't explain what more looked like, but I knew I was different.

I left school at 16 without a single qualification to my name, not one! Most would have resigned themselves to a life with not much hope I didn't, but the world around me did. Everyone and their dog seemed to want to tell me what I should do with my life, all opinions and voices threw at me from all angles, but all pretty much saying the same thing. Go get a job and settle into life.

It sounded like hell! But off I went at sixteen to my first job, I worked in a call centre, and I lasted six weeks. Not because I couldn't do it, I could, but apparently standing up to a manager who was clearly wrong wasn't appropriate and so I was let go. After my short experience of dipping my toe into the working world, I moved to London with my step sister and my now-husband, I was seventeen at the time, and when I think about that now, it's totally crazy. Seventeen moved out and living in London! It was here that I had my eyes opened, I'd walk down Oxford Street and around the Ritz just imagining myself living that life, in the designer shops picking up everything, sipping champagne and celebrating an amazing day.

It opened my eyes to a world I knew existed but had never really been involved with before, I got to see the world through a new pair of eyes, and it further ignited the feeling inside myself that I was born for more. I knew I belonged in those circles; I knew I belonged in that space even though at that moment in time, I couldn't have been further away from it all! I had no job, no money, and no direction at all as to where I was going, I just knew I'd be going somewhere.

At 18 I'd moved back to Wales, but I fell pregnant, queue the disappointing comments and eye rolls, here is the eighteen-year-old who hadn't gone back to education, has no qualifications, no job, and now she's pregnant! Even if they didn't always say it out loud, I knew it's what they were thinking. At our twenty week scan, we were given the news that all was not ok, and what would follow would be weeks and months of specialist appointments and planning for the series of operations our daughter would have to go through when born. She was diagnosed with Hypoplastic Left Heart Syndrome; I don't think I slept from the moment we were told. I'd spend hours just researching and reading through everything they'd given us. What I didn't know at this moment was in a few months down the line, my whole world would change, and the event that triggered me into getting myself to where I am now would take place.

At thirty-two weeks I was given the news that no one ever wants to hear, I'd felt that something wasn't quite right and so I got in touch with my mother as my husband was working shifts and so wasn't at home. My mother suggested we go to the hospital just as a precaution. On arrival at the hospital, I got hooked up to all those machines, and I feared the worst, but then over the monitor came the sound of the heartbeat that I'd heard so many times throughout all the appointments, and I was relieved. I was quickly informed that they weren't happy and had arranged a conference call with all of the consultants and professors that had so far been involved with my case, and they were arranging for delivery to take place. But still, she was ok and so was I, taken off the monitors and told just to relax while they all made their decisions I laid there having no idea what was to come next.

They wanted to have a scan and to take some measurements before they made their final decision on how to progress. I wasn't worried; I'd not long heard the heartbeat, so what was there to worry about, right? But I was wrong, because ten minutes later after lying down for the scan the words that would stay etched in my memory forever were said out loud to us "I'm sorry, but there's no heartbeat!"

And that was that, thirty-two weeks all of those dreams and hopes I'd laid there thinking about, and her life, gone. No one really knows how it feels until it's them; you see it on tv programs and read about it in magazines sometimes, but it never crossed my mind that it would be me, but suddenly that was my reality. That was me, the one who's baby had died. A few days later, I was taken into hospital to deliver her, walking out of the hospital later that day with nothing other than an A5 booklet with prints, pictures, and her hair was nothing short of heartbreaking.

But it would be a completely horrific tragedy, and moment in my life that would lead me to where I am today, it was my life-defining moment.

I wanted more from life; I wanted my life to really mean something, I didn't want to spend my life feeling as if I didn't belong and that I was destined for more but not doing anything. I didn't want to settle, I wanted to live an utterly limitless life, and I wanted the family that I knew I would have one day to live it too, I wanted my daughter's death to stand for something.

And so I started my first business, without a clue what I was doing, with no experience and no help. I just woke up one morning and said I'm doing this!

At the time, I was planning my wedding to my now-husband, and as we didn't have the budget to have everything done for us, or have all the fancy companies, we were doing a lot of it ourselves, DIY. I sat there one morning thinking what if instead of just using this stuff for our wedding, we used it for others too and hired them out. That's what I did overnight I started a wedding and event hire business, I had no money to invest and no experience, but I was about to learn that the business world was and is a complete rollercoaster.

Within six months, we had a full order book and had gone from just a handful of hire items to a whole catalogue. We were so busy we had to turn bookings away, we'd even have people from all parts of the country want us to provide our services to them, everywhere from Norfolk to Newcastle and Scotland it was totally insane! By this point, I also had two kids under 11 months at home, but I didn't let that stop me, my kids were never ever going to be a distraction, and they were never going to be an excuse, they were going to be the reason why I did it all and not the reason I didn't!

So as amazing as things were at that point, I knew we could do more, by this point, my husband had come to work in the business as well. I decided it was time to go bigger, plenty of hotels would provide recommendations of companies you could use and we were listed on most. Still, I had this idea of being the supplier who wasn't just recommended, but that was included in every event the hotels did, corporate, weddings, everything. So I started pitching, I lost count of the number of emails I'd send on a daily basis, but I'd hit all the contact forms and then when I ran out of those I'd find other emails. I didn't have any experience in pitching, and yet here I was, killing it because the responses blew me away, and I was about to land a six-figure contract with a huge hotel chain just over one year in business. I learned that just going for it and doing VS worrying, thinking, and debating was the key, I even pitched to the Queen!

Over the next 12-24 months, I'd grow the company, even more, we had contracts with hotels worldwide, we also had franchisees across the UK, we were booked solid, and things were amazing.

I'm often asked, "What was your secret?" The answer is that I literally just did it. Most people think of an idea or think of something they'd like to do and then spend ten minutes talking themselves out of doing it, but for me, I just did it. I literally just went and got it done. It's one of my most significant pieces of advice for business owners, just go and get it done. Don't give yourself time to get wrapped up in your head and end up talking yourself out of doing something.

Fast forward to 2013, and I hated my life, there I said it! I did, I was working every single day, I never had a weekend off let alone a day off. I couldn't take holidays, I'd lost all sight of the life I was initially building this for.

I had success sure, but the rest was a mess, and I was a mess. I decided drastic action had to be taken, I'd totally fallen out of love with what I did, and actually, I'd come to the realisation, I never loved it anyway. It was just something that was there at the time, it was never a passion, and I certainly never enjoyed it.

So I left it behind, I walked away without a clue as to what was coming next, I knew I was good at business, and I knew I was good at making money. People tell me I have that natural talent for business, I can see and think of things that others just can't, but honestly, I had no clue what to do for myself at that time.

I was a mentor and coach for various organisations at the time, and I genuinely loved it, turns out I wasn't only good at making things happen for myself, I was particularly good at helping others make lots of money, and so it was suggested to me that I turned my passion into a business. At first, I thought they were crazy I mean who on earth was going to follow and buy from me, but the more I thought of it, the more it ticked all the boxes that I'd ever set out for myself, it lit a fire inside of me that I'd never felt before, and so I took the plunge.

In October 2013, I launched my coaching business, The Women's Business Academy, and the rest, as they say, is history, only it wasn't! Queue six months of no sales, I drove myself insane, I mean I knew business, I knew how to make sales, I was shit hot at making sales, and yet I was sucking, and for ages, I couldn't figure out why. I was following all the experts, I had a coach, I was doing the funnels and freebies and webinars and online courses and low-end offerings, it should have been working, but it wasn't.

So six months later I decided enough was enough, I threw out the rule book that others had given me, I threw out all the must-dos and must-haves that the gurus said and I went back to basics, I went to what I knew, and within one week I'd gone from 0 sales to over 15k. I had supercharged my business in just one week! What did I change? I went from online courses and low-end to putting together a high-end package and selling it, I sold out of every space within two weeks.

I quickly grew on that, and my sales just kept rising. Six months later, I had done over 100k in sales, and I had helped my clients do exactly the same thing. No words can describe just how amazing it felt and still does feel to have done it, to have turned it around, and more importantly, be in a position where I was and still do help others do the same.

It sounds cliche, but my coaching business gave me my life and happiness back, high-end selling enabled me to truly unlock the freedom that I had spent so long desiring, in fact, I felt freedom on a level I hadn't ever thought would be possible for me before and it lit me up in a way my first business never did.

Since launching my coaching business back in 2013, I've entered a whole new period of my life, and it's opened doors I never imagined little old me would be walking through. I can remember being shortlisted for my first Great British Entrepreneur Award for Young Entrepreneur Of The Year and thinking, who me?

I'd be lying if I said I never had that voice inside my head going "Who the hell are you to be in this position?" but I don't listen to it and have long learnt to just ignore it. I'm here because I deserve to be, I've earned my place and I'm going to enjoy it.

When I started my coaching business, I genuinely never intended to go back to other types of business. Still, in the past few years, I found myself being called in a few different directions, and when I really dialled into my dream, the word "empire" kept popping up. When I dug into it a bit more I realised that I don't just want to be a coach, I want to own an empire (and yes you might read that thinking REALLY?), but it's true, I'm not your average coach, I'm not your average person. I have big goals, big dreams, and I intend making every one of them my reality. But back to the point after discovering and tuning inside my bigger dreams, I decided it was time to launch some new businesses, but this time I wouldn't be hands-on. So as I write this, I own three companies, including my coaching business, and I genuinely wouldn't have it any other way. I also have a fourth business launching in the next few months.

Side note: If you have big dreams, no matter how ridiculous they may seem, always go after them!

In 2019 I had the honour of being listed as a top 100 UK female entrepreneur one of my proudest moments to date.

But as I write this, I'm actually no longer in the UK, 2019 has been a year of serious growth for me not just professionally but personally. Travel was always a big dream for my family and me, and in the past two years, I have really brought that to life. We've travelled every school holiday and several weeks outside of that. Still, there was a bigger dream I had for myself and my family that I'd been putting off for years for various reasons, most of which being my own bullshit stories, and that dream was to move abroad.

I love my hometown, but I didn't belong there, I felt like my wings were clipped continuously, and I felt suffocated by a place I didn't belong, and 2019 was the year I decided enough was enough. Enough talking about it, enough talking about a better life for my kids (I have three little ones), I decided it was time to do it.

And so in August 2019 as a family, we realised that huge dream I've held since I was a teenager and we moved abroad to Lanzarote in the Canary Islands. An emotional but extremely rewarding process and also a huge goal that I just know younger me is so amazingly proud of us having achieved.

I always say to people that if I can do it then so can you and it's genuinely how I feel if you'd have told twelve years old me that I'd be living here, doing what I do, with the life I have, she'd likely have laughed and sixteen years old me would have been rolling on the floor laughing and hey they'd be right.

I had no qualifications, I had no clue about any of this, but I had a dream, and I wanted my life to mean something. So if I can, that's proof you can too!

Chapter Three

YOUR WHY AND MODEL

*E*veryone says you have to know your why and they're right, knowing your why is important. But it's not just about the whole ¨my kids are my why¨ I mean isn't family largely part of everyone's why?

Your why is so much bigger than that, your why isn't just about who you do this for, but why you do it, it's also about you and the impact you want to make. You might be reading this thinking I don't really want to make an impact I just want to do whatever service or business I run. But whilst you may not want to have this huge mega impact, you do still want to make an impact.

Every business makes an impact; every service creates an impact of some kind on the people they work with. Whether that impact is something small or huge doesn't really matter, but the impact goes way beyond whether you want your name in lights and be this huge name in the industry making an impact, it's about you and those you serve.

So when I talk to people about their why I like to dig deeper than the surface level "My why is my family"

I used to be the person who didn't really understand my why, and it actually led me down the path of creating a business and life I hated, whilst I'm eternally grateful for what my first business enabled me to do and achieve, it also resulted in me being in a terrible place internally and also with the life I was living.

It wasn't until I really started to dig deeper into my why I could see I was always on the wrong path, if my why was just to give my family a better life, then a business that just makes enough money would always have been enough. If I focused on the why of wanting to be successful, then yeah, any business would do, right?

But once I started to dig deeper into what my why was, I realised it wasn't even about what I'd always say my why was.

Sure I wanted to create a better life for my family; of course, I wanted to be successful, but it was about so much more than that.

My why was about those I wanted to serve.

My why was about the life I really wanted to live.

My why was about the world around me.

My why was about who I was connected with.

My why was about the impact I was making.

My why was actually a lot more about me than others, and at first, that felt really selfish, I actually thought I was selfish.

Considering pretty much all you ever see online is:

"My why is my kids."

"My why is my family."

"My why is I want to give my family a better life."

"My why is because I want to retire from my husband."

In 2013 I'd done all of that, and yet I was deeply unhappy with a business I absolutely hated, working with people I genuinely didn't vibe with.

And so when I started to dig back into my why during the period of time where I was trying to figure out what the hell I was going to do with my life, I realised that those things were never really my whys.

Sure they were part of it.

Sure they fuelled me. But they were part of something much bigger.

My unearthed why.

The reason why I never really uttered out loud.

But it was unearthing that real why and claiming that why loud and proud that set me off on a path of non-negotiable creating a business and life that I genuinely love, and that has provided my family with a life I could only have once dreamed of!

And that's why your why is so important but not that surface-level why, not the why that you think is acceptable to society but the why that really fuels you, and it may not be just one thing, I know mine wasn't.

My why is more of an experience for myself, it's a combination of things VS being just one thing that can be summarised into a nice little sentence.

You might roll your eyes when people ask you about your why, and I used to do that until I understood the real importance of it and until I went deeper.

I can remember scrolling through social media and seeing those "What's your why?" questions and reading all the answers, which were just comment after comment of the same old stuff. The stuff that society tells us has to be our why if we're a parent, a partner, a child.

But why will never fuel you and in fact that why can lead us (in my case) down paths that aren't ever going to truly fulfil the why that we have inside of us, it may satisfy the outer why, the one you share with the world but what about the fire that burns inside of you, that dream you hold inside, that vision? That's your why!

All of my clients fill in an onboarding questionnaire, and one of the questions on there asks, what's your why? And I can remember reading one of my first ever clients reply and thinking, that's not really her why!

We got on the call, and I'll be honest. I was a little terrified in exploring this with her (I had all sorts of beliefs pop up), but we were going through different things, and she was telling me all about what she was looking to do. But it was soulless; she sounded empty.

And so I asked, "But what do you really want? Really want, the want, and the why that really lights you up?"

Twenty minutes later, she 'd described something so amazing, and she sounded so excited, and I could just feel her energy, but she said: "That's not for me, though."

Of course, it was for her; she just had not let herself believe it or even consider for a second it could be.

Your why is important but it has to be yours, it has to be what fuels you and yes it may be huge, it may be lightyears away from what you currently think is possible for you but don't shut it down, don't´t ignore it because you think it isn't possible for you. It is, and it's your why, and you should let the world see and experience it!

Struggling to connect with you, why? I hear you; I used to have real big difficulty in connecting with a why that fuelled me; I'd always go back to that safe why the one I thought I should have until I tried something different.

Instead of sitting there with a pen desperately trying to get something to come out, I did a series of different exercises.

First off I wrote out my perfect day, everything from the moment I got up until I went to sleep, what I smelled, how I felt, what I did, what I ate and WOW was that eye-opening, I hadn't really ever realised what I truly wanted my day to look like.

Secondly, I closed my eyes and allowed myself to connect with that inner fire, what fuelled it, what didn't, what did it need? It's funny when most of us think of our why the answer comes from our head but really the true answer to your why lies inside of you, connect to it and allow yourself to hear it!

You may be thinking, what's this got to do with high-end selling? Well, it has everything to do with it because if you're not working in a way that fuels your why and if you're not living a life that lights you up, then you'll end up like 2013 me and I wouldn't want anyone to be there.

Your High-End Business Can Fit With Your Why

One of the biggest reasons why I held myself back from actually selling high-end packages for almost six months was because my why was to create a freedom business, I wanted a freedom life, I wanted to be able to travel and have this amazing life, and I was under the assumption that the only way for me to do that was to run online courses and have it all automated through a funnel.

The issue with that is that it didn't fuel me, hey I love offering online courses but I also really love the personal interaction and equally at the beginning, I was in no position to drive the volume of traffic I needed to make the conversions on those courses.

Six months later, I was no closer to my why, and honestly, I'd even started to go down the route of following a why that wasn't mine (AGAIN I KNOW!)

But I genuinely didn't know how I could make high-end packages fit my why; I believed I couldn't, I was swept up into the mindset of thinking I had to have online courses and funnels and that was it.

Here's the thing though there are no rules, I mean hell you make the rules it's your business and life right, and when I really thought about that I thought you know what who actually says I can't do this!

Re-visiting and re-connecting with that why reminded me that high-end selling would be part of my why, it would fuel me and light me up, and I was sure I could make it fit all of my why and fuel me entirely.

And the result....it could, and it did!

High-end selling is actually a lot more flexible than I think most people realise, see when I normally mention high end selling to people they're like, "oh so I'd be selling a ninety-day package, but I'm not a coach, so that doesn't work for me."

But that isn't how it is at all, you can literally do whatever you desire, and it's about leveraging your time through high-end selling.

Let's say you were a service-based business like a book-keeper or accountant; then you do a lot of hands-on work, in fact, most of your work right now might be hands-on, so high-end selling is about looking at things differently, positioning them differently and taking your hands-on work and packaging it in a high-end way.

This means that you leverage your time whilst drastically increasing your income and, in many cases, work a hell of a lot less too.

The possibilities are endless, and just because you don't know anyone else who does it doesn't mean it isn't possible for you.

I have a client who is a personal trainer but sells out 30k packages four times a year!

It's all in the positioning, which we'll get to later but the point is everyone can create high-end packages and sell them with ease, every business has the possibility to position itself in a high-end way it's largely down to whether you're willing to explore the possibility and for a few minutes allow yourself to create.

But can a high-end offering model enable you to travel?

Absolutely, travelling was a big goal of mine; it was previously something we simply couldn't do first because of money and then because of time and the business I'd created, so travel was a big goal for me, and

I did think that maybe high end selling would restrict me, but actually, it has the opposite effect.

I started to host intensive days in various locations around the world, locations I wanted to travel to, and take my family. So I'd open up intensive day spaces in those locations, but I'd usually restrict it to two days, those two days would not only cover expenses for the whole trip for all of us but would still leave me with over 50% profit, you might be thinking but Jane you had to work two days?

Yes, I did but two days out of 10 wasn't really a huge deal for me, and I saw it as a stepping stone to where I ultimately wanted to be, it opened the doors to that travel lifestyle we desired, and so it was more than worth it.

My point is that there are so many options on how you can actually use high-end packages to kick start that travel lifestyle if that's what you desire.

It's all possible!

But this is why it's essential to connect in with your why and also then look at what model you'll be starting with, which is going to most connect you with your why and start you on the path to living your dream life.

What fuels you?

What lights you up?

What kind of life do you really want to be living?

If you could serve your clients in any way, how would that look?

Let your mind run wild (it's ok to do that, it's where you discover your best ideas!)

What parts of your business that you currently do hands-on can be utilised in a high-end package?

Don't get hung up on the how right now, just allow yourself to explore, explore your why, your business, how you want to work and serve people!

Chapter Four

THE FOUNDATION

*Y*ou might be ready and raring to go and want to start selling these high-end packages right now, and that's the mistake 99% of people make. They skip the foundation, a fundamentally crucial part of their business. They just brush over it without much thought and then wonder a few months down the line why nothing seems to be working for them despite the fact they're showing up etc.

You wouldn't build a house without solid foundations, so why would you build your business on rocky foundations?

Why wouldn't you invest time in the most crucial part?

For most people the reason they don't spend a lot of time here is because it's "boring" it's not the fun making money part right, and I get that but here's the thing, without this part you won't make money anyway!

One of the founding pieces of the foundation is your ideal client, queue eye roll for some I'm sure after all the internet is swamped with the message around the importance of knowing your ideal client and yet still people don't do it!

But unlike the traditional ideal client discovery of answering 15 questions about what they eat and where they shop, I like to do things a little differently, because your ideal client isn't just about knowing what they like and what they do, it's about knowing who makes your soul sing. It's also about knowing who your red flag ideal clients are, and it's also not about figuring your ideal client out on a piece of paper from your own head but rather getting out there.

It's funny everyone knows they need to know their ideal client, and yet 90% of the people I speak to either don't have one, don't get specific enough or worse still don't even like the ideal client they have.

When working with a client, I often hear, "I chose this one as they have money, but I find them really difficult to work with." That, for me, is always a big NO!

There's a myth around the whole, 'if you choose an ideal

client who has money, then they'll easily buy,' and it's one of the biggest myths going because it can't be further from the truth.

First of all, how do you actually know who has money and who doesn't?

How do you actually know how much is in their bank account?

Second of all, just because they have money doesn't mean they see the value in what you do and if they don't see the value the chances of them buying are 1% (very slim!)

People only buy what they value; they're not going to buy just because they have money, and you've decided they're an ideal client of yours based on that.

Some of my best clients are those who didn't have tons of money just sitting in their account; some of my highest paying clients are those who didn't have it!

On the flip side, I've been on sales calls with people who genuinely have had plenty of money just sitting there, and yet they've not bought. Because ultimately, how much they do or don't have isn't a true indicator of whether they'll be an ideal client of yours.

And trust me, you do not want to be stuck with a client you don't like, and neither do you want to have an audience filled with people you don't vibe with either!

I've been there, I've got the t-shirt, and I wouldn't recommend it to anyone, you'll feel as if you're having the life sucked out of you and all they want is more blood.

You're worth so much more than settling for an ideal client you think you have to have because you've concluded that they have money and so will be an easy sell. They won't be, and if by some miracle they do say yes, you might just wish they hadn't!

In fact, the whole ideal client thing tends to be skewed online to just figuring out who that ideal client is, but what about who the ideal client isn't?

Knowing who we don't want to work with is just as important as knowing who we do want to work with, why? Because like above, there's nothing worse than being stuck working with people or surrounded by those we dread having to speak to.

That's not a business that lights you up, that's not living limitlessly, that's selling out for a sale! And none of us want that, right?

Is your ideal client really that important?

100% it is, without it, you won't be able to create copy that converts, you won't know what they want and so won't be able to create things they want to buy, you won't know where they hang out, and so marketing can be tricky, without knowing your whole house falls down!

But on saying that, sitting there answering twenty-one questions about your ideal client isn't the way to go either. I'll let you in on a secret; you can actually know a lot less about your ideal client to get started and make sales while figuring the rest out!

Who your ideal client is and who it isn't - The first step

I mentioned how knowing who it is and who it isn't is just as important as each other, and it's easily the first step in the foundation of your ideal client.

This isn't the part where I tell you to write out twenty-one questions about your ideal client and tell me where they shop for their weekly food (unless of course you help them with food and in which case that might be useful)

What do you actually need to know about your ideal client?

Do you really need to know how many Starbucks they buy a month?

Do you need to know where they buy their shoes?

Think about what you actually need to know, and I'm also talking the basic stuff, the things that mean you could go out there next week and find these ideal clients and actually start talking to them in a way that has them seeing you're someone they need and hey if that's knowing what they had for breakfast then find that out, but if it isn't, don´t have sleepless nights trying to answer it.

The basics you need to know are:

Who are they?

Where do they hang out (personally and for business, if applicable)?

What are they currently googling looking for answers to?

What do they want?

What´is potentially keeping them awake at night?

Who do I really want to work with?

And that is about it, to begin with, do you need to know

more, I mean you could but I've seen people drive themselves crazy for months trying to find out every single detail about their ideal clients and in my opinion it's wasted. Because the real answers you're looking for, the real things you need to know about your ideal client very rarely come from answering twenty-one questions about them in your own head.

They come from you working, talking, engaging, and showing up in front of them.

They come from you actually being with them, in their space, or having them in yours.

They come from you starting.

The real deeper valuable things you need to know about your ideal client aren't going to come from you sitting there on your own scrolling through social media trying to figure it out; it's going to come from you getting out there and in some cases working with them.

One of my clients in the nutrition field had spent eight months trying to discover her ideal client, she could tell me all of these assumptions she had about them, she could list off how many dogs they had and kids and where they liked to holiday, but the real important stuff, the stuff that would actually get them converting and buying, she didn't know.

I got her to answer the five questions above, and she said, what's next?

My reply, you're going to create content and get out there!

She thought I was crazy.

But she did it.

Four weeks later, she had active people in her audience, new leads, and she had even made two high-end sales!

She'd spent eight months with all this information about her ideal client and had got nowhere, in four weeks not only had she made progress, but she actually discovered more out about her ideal client than she knew before and not just any random rubbish but real information, things that actually mattered and were going to help her make even more sales.

The other part of your ideal client is really knowing what you actually enjoy doing. What lights you up, what would you love to do day in day out with your clients and your work? It's important to be doing work that fuels us, not work that de-fuels us and takes us away from living our limitless life.

Ultimately you won't discover what you need to know about your ideal client by just staying in your head, you'll discover it by getting out there with the basics you know and building from there!

But what about who your ideal client isn't, I mentioned that being important and it is not so much for them but for you.

By knowing who your ideal client isn't you can keep a lookout for those red flag signs, you can also make sure you're filtering out the not ideal clients in your copy, sales process etc.

If you've previously worked with clients, then you can use them in this exercise, but if not, then you can think of friends, work colleagues, people in your family, or your circle.

Have three columns: People I like, People I neither like or dislike, People I don't vibe with

Then think of people and put them in each one.

Once you've filled the columns, start to think about why you put them in those areas.

Do they have a personality that vibes/doesn't vibe with you?

Do they make excuses, or do they have this drive that motivates you?

That'll give you a good idea of the type of person you don't vibe with and who wouldn't be an ideal client, but the other part of this is also looking at what you perhaps don't enjoy helping people with or doing.

Just like above where we looked at what lights you up, what doesn't?

What would you hate to spend your days doing with people?

What do you not enjoy helping people with?

Perhaps there's a type of condition, business, or career you don't enjoy helping people with. This is the part where you get honest with yourself on what that is.

The part of the ideal client that exercise that sells

Sure, you might by now know who they are, where they hang out, and the types of things they want help with or struggle with, but what about the part that gets them buying?

You might think it's just about knowing that right, who are they, what do they want, and where can I show up selling it to them? And in part, you'd be correct, but it's not the only part of it.

Have you guessed what it is?

"What triggers them into buying, and what are their buying habits?"

For most people, there will be a trigger, something that happens, they see, or they experience even if that means they pull that trigger and buy.

It's important to know this because you will want to factor it into your marketing, sales process, and copy.

But people just buy when they want it?

Some do, but not all.

Sometimes people will sit thinking about it, complaining about it or even hovering over the sales button for days before they buy, it could be something they experience for months if not years before they do anything. Why is that?

Because for some people or in most cases, actually there's a trigger that triggers them into buying, into taking action, to stop talking and start doing.

For some people, it's an event.

For others, it can be a trauma.

For others, a change in their life.

What would it be for your ideal clients?

What's the trigger?

What takes them from looking, complaining, and not doing, to pulling that trigger and saying yes?

When you know what triggers them, usually, you can look to adjust your marketing and sales processes to really speak and get in front of the people who are ready to pull that trigger right now.

The next part of knowing what converts your ideal clients is also understanding their buying habits; too often, I see people selling on Facebook when their ideal clients don't buy there. In some cases, their ideal clients have a profile there for sure, but do they spend time on it, use it, or do they use it to stay in touch with family?

You're going to find selling high-end or selling anything easier when you actually know how to get in front of them in the spaces where they actually are and actually buy!

Where do they usually buy?

Do they go to Facebook to make purchases in this area?

Do they look for recommendations on LinkedIn?

Do they head straight to Pinterest?

This isn't the case that you'll pigeon hole yourself into one space (we'll get to that in some of the other chapters) but it is a case of having the full picture on your ideal client's triggers and buying habits so that you can achieve maximum return from your marketing and sales processes.

These two things aren't things you'll necessarily find out by figuring it out yourself; these are more often than not going to be discovered once you're out there in front of them, engaging with them and in some cases actually selling to them.

So don't worry if you don't have the answers right now you really don't need to but certainly for moving forward to the point where you can scale then knowing these two things will be an important part of your scaling process.

Ultimately with your ideal client, I'd have fun with it, imagine yourself being able to work with these people day after day, imagine how it would feel to speak to them, engage with them and create for them.

Does it light you up? If yes, you're on the right track, if no then connect in with what you want a little bit more.

Also, don't get wrapped up in the beliefs your brain may throw at you around "these people won't buy" or "how would you even get in front of them" anything and everything is possible once you know who they are!

Chapter Five

THE HIGH-END PACKAGE

> *You don't get paid for the hour, you get paid for the value you bring to the hour!*
>
> — *JIM ROHN*

If I just stick an expensive price tag on it, then that means it's high-end, uh no!

I know it's what a lot of people think, but it doesn't really work like that, a high-end package is a little more than that, I mean you could just go and stick a high price on something, but you won't make sales, and we're here actually to sell these high-end packages, right?

Of course, no one wants a high-end package that no one buys and the secret to actually getting people to buy your high-end packages is to put them together in a way that makes them irresistible to your ideal clients.

And then I guess the question of what actually makes something high end comes in?

The answer isn't necessarily straight forward; there isn't a firm set of rules that says this is what makes a package high end or not, in fact, if you were to google this question you'd see thousands of results all with vastly different answers.

I think ultimately what makes something high end is dependant on the purchaser and the one selling; it depends on the purpose, the outcome, the audience and much more. To say that there's only one thing or one package that could ever be high end doesn't work and to say that a package has to include set things to be high-end doesn't work either for the same reasons.

With any type of package, the secret to it actually being successful is that it has what your ideal clients want and need, the same principle applies to high-end selling.

I have various high-end packages, all different, all include slightly different things, all delivered through slightly different experiences, but they're still high end.

But having said all of that putting together a high-end

package is pretty simple, it doesn't include needing to tie yourself in knots or figure out how you're going to hire a yacht for a month; it's actually a lot simpler than that.

Always focus on where the aeroplane is going and not the aeroplane itself.

I'm sure you've heard the saying before "sell them what they want and then give them what they need" well "sell where the aeroplane is going and not the aeroplane itself" is the same principle, and it's the starting point of putting a high-end package together.

One of the things that makes a package high end is the value that the package provides. It's actually crazy how much of a difference positioning towards value makes when it comes to packages and the success of them selling.

A client in the health and wellness sector came to me full of frustration; she knew that her audience needed what she was selling and yet no one was buying her packages, she said none of them could afford anything. In fact, at this point, she believed she needed to find some wealthy clients to buy from her as she thought that her targeting was wrong.

I challenged this, and together we took her offerings and

created two high-end packages. One was 5k another was 8k; she wasn't convinced.

I can clearly remember her words "Jane if these people won't pay even $90 for something really small on what planet are they going to pay these prices?"

But I knew that her issue wasn't that her audience couldn't afford it; her problem was a positioning one. Her package did not show value; her packages didn't speak to the want they had, she was selling what she thought they needed and also selling the service she provided VS what the service does for them.

At the end of the call, after we had put together the packages and some marketing, she was left with a challenge for the week, sell one of these high-end packages. She laughed, she left the call laughing, and she honestly wasn't sure about this, secretly I think she was looking forward to coming back next week and saying "see Jane I told you they couldn't afford anything!"

But she didn't come back the next week and say that, in fact, seventy-two hours later she left me a voice message telling me she had sold one, by the time we spoke the following week she had sold three!

Her very first buyer of a high-end package was someone

who had previously said no to a really low-cost offer of hers.

But this time she bought, she bought something that was over 10x more than something previously offered. Why? Why did that happen?

It actually happens more than people realise, when people receive money as an objection they automatically assume it means someone can't afford it and yes, sometimes this is the case, but there's also plenty of occasions where it isn't the case. The reason they say no is because they don't see the value in the offer.

And how do people see value? They see the value by focusing on the want that they have.

And that's the want how they see it, not you selling them what you think they need but you selling them what it is they say they want.

So your starting point when putting together a high-end package is to look at the want, what's the want your ideal clients have?

What's the value they desire?

That's the focus of your high-end package, that's what you're going to be selling!

The kitchen sink doesn't belong in a high-end package!

The first high-end package I put together I threw everything and the kitchen sink into it, why? Because I made the mistake of thinking that's how you show value.

This is a really common myth people believe in; I have to show that this package is worth the amount I'm going to be selling it for so I need to cram it full of everything because more stuff = worth more.

No.

It's as simple as that it doesn't work and actually it can have the opposite effect.

Have you ever been at the end of a sales pitch or maybe even just reading some things online and by the end of it your head is hurting, and you don't have a clue what this person has tried to say, do or sell to you?

That will have happened because they've thrown everything and the kitchen sink at it, it creates so much noise that the value actually gets lost.

And so you can have a package full of every single thing you could possibly think of, and yet people still won't see the value.

Which sounds crazy, surely the more it includes, the more valuable it becomes?

That only works if they value the individual things but for most people that isn't the case, what they value is the want, and so if your package suddenly has everything and the kitchen sink in it then it actually devalues it because it creates so much noise that they can longer focus on the value.

The other thing that happens is people can feel really overwhelmed, if they're staring at this really long list of things that are included their brain automatically goes "wow that's a lot" and if they feel overwhelmed they won't go any further with it.

Likewise, if you don't put anything in it, then people will be like, so I just magically get this want?

And of course, that isn't the case; they will receive things as part of the package, whatever that means for you and what you do.

But it's having the balance; it's making sure they have what they need in the package without taking them into a space where they feel overwhelmed and have all this noise that detracts from the value of the package.

Your package has to fit your vision!

There's nothing worse than building a business you end up hating, take it from someone who's been there it isn't fun, and it isn't pretty! But it happens a lot; I've lost count of the number of people who come to work with me who tell me how they hate what they've created or are trying to create, sometimes it's a classic square peg round hole situation.

In the online world, there's so much noise that it's easy to get swept up in this idea that there's only a certain number of ways you can do anything. Want to live a laptop lifestyle? Then you have to do online courses. Want to be a bookkeeper? Then you can only provide this type of package! The reality is actually quite the opposite.

Who says you have to do it that way?

Who says you can't look outside of the box that you think you have to fit into?

Who says you can't get really creative?

In reality, no one, and if they did, it doesn't matter the only person's opinion that matters is yours and the only set of rules that really matter are your own too.

When I left my first business I wanted to create a life and business I truly loved, and part of that for me was travelling, long term it was also moving abroad, but travelling was that first step. I wanted to see the world and take my kids with me, I thought the way to do it was online courses, and I spent six months trying to do that.

It wasn't until I embraced what my soul truly wanted at that moment in my life did I actually make any of it happen. I built a six-figure business within six months, and I didn't sell a single online course during that time, and neither did I work 24 hours a day seven days a week, in fact, I worked less than I ever had and travelled more than I could have imagined at that time in my life.

The reality is that when it comes to your high-end package, you can be as creative as you want. I wanted to travel, and so I thought how can I create a package that enables me to do that, I decided to run in-person intensive days, but instead of hosting them in my backyard, I hosted them in places I wanted to visit. I was literally being paid to travel!

The box you think might exist for you doesn't, you can be as creative as you want, but it has to be fuelled by you, for you and for the life you desire to live.

If you want to travel, then how can you potentially create a package that enables you to do just that?

If you crave more in-person experiences, then how can you create a package that enables you to do just that?

You might be reading this thinking, but someone in my profession doesn't do any of that...oh really? Maybe they haven't because they've thought the exact same thing!

I had a client who was a virtual assistant, but she craved travel and more in-person experiences, but she didn't want to create an online course either. I asked her what she'd really love to do and she soon described an amazing experience where she'd meet in person with a client and plan out systems, automation, content and strategy for six or twelve months.

I asked her why she believed she couldn't do that, and aside from "I've never seen anyone else do that" there wasn't a real objection.

Twelve months later she had a waiting list for her days, hosted in various locations worldwide and she had even moved into offering retreats and had sold her first three retreats out. She had literally gone from selling her VA services for $30 an hour to hitting over $100k in sales in just 12 months.

What changed? She sold what she wanted; she created packages with her ideal clients wants in mind but didn't decide how to deliver them based upon an invisible box that she had put herself in. More importantly, she was delivering them in a way that enabled her to live out her vision.

People think that selling something is all about having what people want and yes to a certain degree it is but you also have to want to do what you're selling. You actually have to believe in it, be excited about it and want to deliver it. Your energy is everything when it comes to sales.

Think about what you desire in life, the life you desire and the experiences you desire, think about how you'd love to work with your ideal clients, and how you'd love to deliver that. That's what you need to be creating, that's what you need to be selling!

Do I need a yacht?

The first high-end package I put together in my coaching business legit did include a yacht experience, champagne dinner and a personal stylist!

Sounds fancy right? And it was, but it was totally NOT what my ideal clients valued and actually didn't add a single thing to the experience other than make it expensive. Which you might be thinking is precisely what you need to do, how else do you make it a high-end experience if there isn't some fancy high-end experience included, but you'd be wrong.

Because actually throwing the fancy stuff in there as an experience IF it isn't of value to your ideal clients and actually adds to the experience will just mean they look at it and go well that's expensive for a weekend on a yacht!

They'll be focusing on the element of the package that stands out the most to them, which will be this really expensive experience you've included in your pursuit of making it high-end.

I didn't sell any of those packages by the way, not one, everyone made the same comment.

"I can't afford that."

"Not right now, I'm not in a position to do it."

So I changed it, threw out the yacht and champagne dinner and instead thought about what they would truly value, what would really enhance the experience for them, and I replaced it with that.

The same people who said no then said yes, the same price, same want but with an experience that mattered to them, one they valued, one that actually fitted.

The reality is that the yacht experience and champagne dinner made them feel as if it wasn't for them, they weren't in a position where they were even contemplating that life right now, and so when they saw it included, it took them away from the real value and instead made them feel like it wasn't for them.

You don't need a yacht unless it's something that lights you up but also would make your ideal clients go YES!

You don't need to give them diamonds unless it makes sense to you and them!

High-end doesn't mean ridiculously rich and luxurious, not always, is it sometimes? Sure, of course, it is if it's relevant to your ideal clients but remember that not everyone values or wants it for that matter.

When thinking of the experience element of your high-end offer focus on your ideal client, ask yourself what they'd actually value, what would actually enhance this experience for them.

Sometimes you might even find that it's the simplest of things that make the most impact for them!

You'll get the, yes when you've made the package so damn valuable it's screaming at them that they need this and you don't always achieve that through dazzling them.

Remember that they have to want the package you're selling right now and not see it as a luxury that they'll do further down the line when they're in a different position.

Don't focus on the price!

It's a high-end package; how can I not focus on the price?

Focusing on the price is going to lead you to create from all the wrong places, and it's likely going to mean you make all the mistakes that people usually make and result in not making sales.

"I want to sell something that's 5k what do I need to put in it?"

For example, this isn't the way to do it, you could ask yourself what may be 5k valuable to your audience but don't ever create from the price. Creating from the price means you'll fall into all the pitfalls I mentioned above.

Throwing everything and the kitchen sink into it.

The package being so noisy they can't see the value.

Getting wrapped up in the money energy yourself.

Remember that a high-end package isn't about the price, but the value and experience your ideal clients will be receiving, in whatever way you feel lit up in delivering it.

Focus on your ideal client.

Focus on the want.

Focus on what you want to create.

That's the winning secret to creating high-end packages that sell, don't fall into feeling the pressure of the figure.

Chapter Six

THE KEY TO NOT BEING THE BEST KEPT SECRET

"Marketing"

*Y*ou could have the most amazing services and offerings, you could be the best coach in the entire world but if people don't know you actually exist how would they ever know they can buy from you?

It's curious because in a day and age where we're marketed to almost every single day it's crazy to think that as business owners you wouldn't be marketing and yet that's largely what happens to so many business owners I speak to.

Marketing is necessary; it doesn't really matter which way you approach it; marketing is absolutely crucial when it comes to getting leads. If the world doesn't know you exist how on earth will they ever know they need or want your services?

The first time I marketed I didn't have a clue what I was doing, I'd never done a degree let alone a marketing one, at nineteen I hadn't ever stepped foot into the marketing world and yet suddenly I needed to market.

The funny thing is for the first six months of my business; I didn't think I was marketing, all I was doing was sharing content and having conversations, was that actually marketing?

Surely marketing is all this fancy stuff, huge campaigns and for big business, right? Wrong.

Marketing is everything from having a conversation right through to those big campaigns. Still, marketing is necessary for every business big or small; without it, your ideal clients simply won't know you exist.

In my first business, I could never understand why people complicated marketing, why they were afraid of it so much, until I launched my coaching business and then woah did I get what they were saying. No matter how you dress it up marketing your own services or marketing yourself as a coach is different, and that is ultimately why people tend to overcomplicate marketing.

Not because it is complicated but rather because of what they're making marketing mean. Marketing is the gateway to getting leads and sales, but it's also the gateway to putting yourself out there, and if your business is you then that also means the fear of being judged or saying something someone doesn't agree with comes in. Suddenly marketing isn't just getting a lead, but it's part of something much bigger.

But none of that is true and ultimately if you give all your power to the fear of those who won't then you miss out on being able to serve, help and work with those who need and want what you offer! Not only that but by giving your power to the fear of those who never will, you also miss out on opening the doors to your dreams too, is the fear of being judged really worth that?

99.9% of the time, what we worry about never happens anyway, and boy do people worry about all sorts when it comes to marketing.

Trust me, the chances of any of it happening are really slim and hey if they do will it actually matter all that much? Probably not, I can assure you the world won't end if someone sees your marketing and doesn't agree with it; after all, you're not for everyone.

Marketing isn't a cookie-cutter approach.

I should likely run for cover here as there'll be plenty of people who disagree with me, but I firmly believe that marketing that actually works and gets a return doesn't come from a cookie-cutter approach, after all, what works for one doesn't always work for someone else.

Some of the communities I spend time in get flooded with questions from people like "Should I use google ads?", "Will I get a return on XYZ?"

And then it's followed by hundreds of different comments; some say yes it'll work, it worked for me, others saying no it'll never work, it didn't work for me. But in reality, the only real actual answer should be "it depends".

Because that is the thing with marketing, it does depend.

It depends on your business, your market, your budget, your self.

Just because it worked for Doris, the florist doesn't mean it'll work for Grace, the personal trainer!

I love Facebook, and billions of people are on it but believe it or not, it's not the place for everyone to market, some people simply won't see a return there as their ideal clients don't use it, it seems unbelievable, but it's true.

The key with marketing is to have a marketing strategy that is going to get you the best return for your business and to do that the marketing strategy has to fit you and your business, it has to fit where your ideal clients will be.

It's all about the conversions.

Likes, they look lovely and all, but they don't mean a whole lot if they're not converting into sales which is ultimately what your marketing needs to do for you. Marketing isn't about getting you the most likes it should be about getting you the return you're looking for, and to do that it has to be a fit for you.

But where do you start?

How do you actually know what will convert?

The key to a marketing strategy that converts is two-fold, the first part is being in the right places and the second being in them with the right content.

So many people don't see a return from their marketing

because they're either in the wrong place with the right stuff or in the right place with the wrong stuff, resulting in nothing working for them.

I mentioned above how not everyone is on Facebook, and it's true, but equally not everyone uses Facebook in the same way either. I have elderly relatives with Facebook accounts who do nothing more than go on, view some pictures, and log back off again. To assume that everyone uses everything the same way leads you down a path of creating a marketing strategy that doesn't work.

The first part of creating a strategy that converts is understanding your ideal clients and knowing all of the places they hang out and how they use them.

They may well be on Facebook but do they spend their time in groups? You might but do they?

It's often a mistake people make with marketing, because they use groups they assume everyone else does as well, but in reality that isn't the case, you do, but they may not, and if they don't then putting your time and energy into marketing there isn't going to see you get a return.

Understand where they hang out but more importantly, when it comes to social media understanding how they use that platform. What do they do on there? How do they interact and use it?

Once you've listed out all the areas in which you know they hang out you're halfway to having the basis of your marketing strategy sorted out and being able to answer the "where should I market question?" But it isn't the only part of it; there's often a whole other side that people overlook when it comes to where they should market, and that is understanding where they're currently looking!

Where do your ideal clients currently go to buy hire or get help with issues? Where is their first port of call?

For example, if I'm looking to hire someone for my business the first place I go to is my network for recommendations, but then if I'm redecorating my house, I'll go to Pinterest first likewise if I'm looking for help with something I'll hit google first.

Why is knowing any of that important?

Because by knowing the answer to those questions, I can then figure out how I can use them to get directly in front of my ideal clients in the areas in which I know they're already looking.

Why reinvent the wheel?

If you know where they'll be, then you just need to be there in front of them in those spaces! It's actually one of the simplest ways to ensure that you're showing up in front of them in a space where you will get a return, and yet most people don't know the answer to it.

Where to market is focused on your ideal client, not you, they may well be in the same spaces you are but don't assume it, make sure you know it for sure otherwise you're going to be marketing in all the wrong places and seeing no return on your time or money.

Another critical thing to remember with this is understanding where the different platforms and methods of marketing fit in your processes, for example, I see lots of people marketing on their Facebook page but their ideal clients aren't actively looking for them on Facebook. They're not using the platform in that way, they'll follow you, but only once they know you exist. You should be marketing to drive people to your Facebook page and then understand that the marketing you do on there may be different to what you do elsewhere as they're further into your world by this point.

Clarity around where things fit in your process is essential, which is why knowing how they use different platforms is important, once you know you can then ensure you're marketing in the right spaces with the right content.

The "with what?"

You know where to market, but what do you market with?

I like to think of this as making a sandwich; you don't make a sandwich with just one piece of bread, you make a sandwich with various layers, and that's exactly how your marketing should work. Your marketing shouldn't be one layer.

When we think about why people buy various reasons come into play, they buy because it's what they want, but they also buy because they feel you're the person for them and they also trust you. You won't achieve that in your marketing by using just one layer. You'll achieve that by using multiple layers and consistently might I add.

What layers you have in your marketing may well depend on your audience and what you're selling, but for me, the main ones that everyone should have are:

- Engagement
- Positioning as the expert/the one who has what they want

- Know like and trust factor
- Objection handling

They're the main ones for me because without those your sandwich won't be in a position to convert and bring you leads, and it doesn't have to be complicated either, like everything it's as simple or as difficult as you choose to make it.

Engagement - There are so many different ways that you can bring engagement into your marketing. You can have them reply to you, ask them a question, ask their thoughts on something, have content that is easy for them to share.

It's about keeping things simple; I've seen people who post these really long ridiculous questions that aren't quick and easy for people to engage with and then they wonder why no one is engaging with them. Your engaging part of your marketing should be quick, easy and simple for people to engage with. The goal is to have them engaging with you in some way, so they get into the habit of actually engaging with you.

Positioning as having what they want - Engaging content is important, but it isn't all you need, in fact, if all you have is engaging content then you'll likely end up with an audience that loves to engage but buys nothing.

For them to buy, they have to see you as having what they want and being the expert for them. So having content that positions you in that way is important, videos, blogs, posts, lives I mean there are various different ways you can do this on multiple different platforms. The key thing to remember is that you're positioning the content in a way that it speaks to their want, struggles, issues.

Know like and trust factor - If people feel as if they don't know you, they won't buy and if people feel as if they don't trust you, then they won't buy either. When selling high-end, this is a very crucial and important part. People have to know you, trust you and feel as if they'd actually like to buy from you. Case studies or social proof is a great way to help with the trust factor and side note, no you won't be showing off and if anyone does see it and think that, then they weren't an ideal client anyway. Sharing your own story, sharing your likes and dislikes, opinions on things are all things that can go a long way in building the know like and trust factor.

Objection handling - Look people will have objections but if you can deal with them before they become a lead then even better and the thing to also keep in mind is that people can have objections about even taking the first step and saying they're interested. But how do you handle objections before they've even said them out loud? The same way you'd deal with anything you hit it head-on, if you know one of their objections might be "I don't have time to do this" or "This isn't for someone in my position" create content that directly shows them why that objection isn't correct and help them overcome it.

How often and exactly how you do each one depends entirely on the platform and your audience. It drives me insane when people say that posting five times is a must when, in reality, that isn't true for everyone. Less focus on how often and more focus on what you're showing up with is really the key with this. You could show up five times a day with a motivational quote, but the chances of you seeing a return from that are pretty slim.

Create your sandwich, what can you do on the different platforms that has all the layers above covered?

Unless you want to train them to 'not buy', you need to do this!

You may have noticed above I didn't mention selling and there's a good reason for that because selling isn't necessarily in the sandwich but rather the stick that goes through the centre keeping it all together.

Without selling, without actually saying to people, "hey

come and take the next step" none of the above layers really work to their maximum potential.

Yes, you'll have some people reach out to you but not always and not everyone will, in fact, you'll be leaving a lot of sales on the table by not letting them know they can take the next step.

When we're building our audience, we're often training them in how to engage with us and what to expect. Not letting them know they can buy often results in having an audience that is all engaged with the freebies but then disappears the minute you randomly do mention buying something.

"If you just show the value, they'll buy" yes if you show the value they will, but you also have to be letting them know they can buy too otherwise the showing the value doesn't result in sales.

I've seen people spend six months or more building value, and then finally they offer something, sure they'll make sells because they've spent all this time building and giving value and yet they don't make a single one. Why?

Because more often than not they've trained them into expecting not to buy, and so when they suddenly ask for it it's like WOAH what's going on here!

The real kicker is that there'll also be people in your audience who you're giving all this value to who go off and buy from someone else, and yes that happens a lot!

I can remember doing a sales call with someone who had mentioned how there are people in their audience who love their stuff, but after five months hadn't bought anything and then they found out they'd hired someone else and they couldn't understand why. But I could, and one question showed exactly why it had happened "Had you let them know that they could buy from you?" the answer, "no I was afraid they'd think I was just being salesy."

But the thing to remember is the whole being salesy is a belief you're creating (we will get onto that in the next chapter). By buying into the belief you have that's telling you you can't ask for the sale, you can't let them know, which means that the people you're showing value to end up buying elsewhere, they buy from the person who has asked, who has let them know!

It's a myth to say you have to build value for months before selling and you'll also be leaving leads and sales on the table if you never let them know you have something for sale.

So the sales in your marketing is the stick, you should be

talking about what you have available, you should be letting these people take the next step because honestly if they don't, will they ever actually change, get the result or get help with whatever it is you do just by following your free content? Probably not. If you really want to serve, then selling is a must!

Don't rewrite their words.

Yes, you need to sell, and you need to let them know you have something they want or need but to do that you have to actually be speaking to them, to that want or need and not rewriting their words, so it fits from your expert point of view.

It comes back to selling where the aeroplane is going and not the aeroplane itself, the same principle in your sales marketing applies. They have to be able to see that it's for them clearly; the language you use is so important.

The language you use is what's going to make the difference between them saying yes or no.

Between them being excited or not.

Between them really wanting this or scrolling right past, paying no attention.

People spend hours staring at their computer screens

trying to figure out what to say, how to say it, how to write it in a way that they'd convert. But the answers to all of that is usually staring them in their face.

It's usually been said to them over and over again.

It's usually something that's been mentioned in a conversation.

You just need to write, create and speak in a way that speaks directly to what they've already told you. Paying attention and really listening is key to high-end selling and it's key when writing copy too when creating marketing content. Because all you need to do is write it in a way that speaks to them.

And how do you speak to them? By repeating their words back to them, not by making them fancy, not by being special, just by saying what they've already said, what they're thinking.

A client of mine who does life coaching showed me her marketing on our first call, and after looking at it and reading it over and over, I was still none the wiser what it was for.

Did it sound fancy? Sure

Did it look good? Yep.

But I'll be damned if I had a clue what she was selling or why I'd want to work with her, and that's the problem, that's what happens when people think they need to have fancy words or be creative or shout the loudest with their marketing, it ends up making no sense or not being clear which means your ideal clients have no clue that this is for them.

I tore it all up and asked her to imagine herself sitting opposite her ideal client; she knows what her ideal client is asking for, looking for and feeling. What would she say to them? How would she describe what she was selling to them?

She changed her whole marketing to reflect that conversation, and she made sales. She actually made sales from content for the first time ever.

And all she did was change what she was saying, instead of changing words, shouting at people or trying to sound fancy she spoke to them. To their problems, their wants, using the words they use to describe where they're at.

That's all you ever need to do, speak to them not at them, speak to how they feel not how you think they should feel and speak to how they describe things not how you think they should be described instead.

The other thing to keep in mind when it comes to this is that your copy in your marketing is also going to help you attract that higher quality of lead, you need to ensure you're specific in who you're speaking to. If you don't want to speak to time wasters, then don't use language that speaks to them, if you only want to attract people who are at this point in their life, then make sure you make that clear in your copy.

One of the biggest reasons why people don't attract those high-quality leads is because they're not specific, because they're not clear with their language, they're not calling in exactly who do they do want whilst making clear exactly who this isn't for.

If you want a higher quality of lead then be very clear with who it is and isn't for, let them know, you can't blame them if you haven't made it clear to them in the first place!

To price or not to price.

This must be a question that gets debated in people's heads right across the globe daily, the question of putting the price or not putting the price.

For every person who says you should, you'll find the same number of people who say you shouldn't and now

I'm going to throw my recommendation out there, but actually, I sort of sit on the fence a little.

I don't think there is a right or wrong way, for some people putting the price works for them for others it doesn't, but there are some things I think people should take into consideration before they make their decision.

Often people decide not to put the price out of fear, fear that they'll scare people off and there's plenty of people who would agree with that "Don't put the price because you'll scare them off wait until you have them on a call where you can show value".

I personally believe this falls into a negative mindset and one born out of fear. The fact is that if you've created your package correctly and write your copy based upon your ideal client and their language, if you're speaking to them, then you should have been able to show the value without any problem and your ideal clients won't be scared off by the price. If they're scared off by the price, are they even an idea client of yours?

The idea that numbers scare people off is crazy; there's people out there selling 50k packages with prices listed on their sales pages and they convert people without even getting on a call. If they can, why would you be scaring everyone off by putting the price?

I really dislike the whole putting the price scares people off, I truly believe that it gives fear a power that it shouldn't have and you're also essentially telling the world that you're not that confident in your own value and that you expect to attract people who will be tough to convert.

Because not putting the price means you are more likely to attract people who will be tougher to convert, they're not fully prepared on the call, they have no idea if this is something that's doable for them or not and so your conversions are likely to be lower than if you have the price up there.

The idea that people are an easier sell when they don't know the price is a myth; in fact, your sales calls will become a whole lot easier when they do know the price!

Equally, do you know how many people will close it down and not take the next step because the price isn't listed? I'll let you know a secret; it's quite a large number. There's a whole percentage of the population and your ideal clients who'll see no price and automatically assume they can't afford it even though it may well be something that's easily affordable for them.

Not having the price listed can actually work against you

as well as for you, and so it isn't as simple to say hide the price, and you'll make more sales. If you weigh it all up and in my own experience I'd say hiding the price does the exact opposite, and actually putting the price increases your sales and the quality of leads that you attract.

Everyone wants to attract a higher quality of lead and putting the price or not can actually have a big reflection on whether you do that, in my opinion, you're more likely to attract high-quality leads when your price is listed.

But that being said I think it does come down to what's best for you, if that's not putting the price then don't but please don't not put the price because you buy into a fear that people will be put off and you'll scare them off. Don't give your fear that power and don't give that signal out to the world, own your value and expect to attract people who can and will pay your prices regardless of what they are!

This is a missing piece for 99% of people!

Have you ever seen someone online, one minute they're nowhere and the next it's as if they've exploded on the scene and are selling like hotcakes?

Well technically I was one of them, I went from 0 to 40k

in under 30 days, and then I hit six figures within six months!

But you see these people, and you wonder what their secret is, here you are no further forward, and they're effortlessly selling high end like no one else's business. What gives? What's the actual deal and what strategy are you missing out on that they seem to have?

Well, it's a secret I'm about to let you know, it's the C-word!

No not Christmas.

Not chocolate

And definitely not that one!

But Collaborations.

One small (ok, medium-sized) word, but a powerful one and one that can skyrocket your results and high-end sales.

Collaborations were a fundamental part of my quick growth, not only did they help me financially with sales, but they also helped me go from 0 to 1000 on my list in under four weeks.

But why? Why are they so powerful?

Above I mentioned the sandwich, the different elements that need to be in your marketing and also I talked about getting in front of them where your ideal clients already are, and collaborations work because they tick all of those boxes and they tick them quicker than you could manage on your own.

Collaborations mean you get directly in front of your ideal clients in spaces they already are, no guessing if they're there you know they are, you know they're in that space.

As they're already in that audience if you're put in front of them, they already trust you on a level that they wouldn't yet if they randomly found you online. Someone else is saying "hey this person can be trusted, so I'm putting them in front of you."

You can engage with them in a way that you don't necessarily get to do when you find them online randomly; they engage better because they already trust you more.

The thing I love about collaborations is that there's no box, you can be as creative as you want with them. Webinars were the done thing back when I launched my coaching, but you can do giveaways, summits, events, trainings, IG takeovers, the possibilities are endless!

Collaborating is the key to skyrocketing, all you need to do is figure out who already has your ideal client in their audience and then get engaging with them, get connected and start booking those collaborations in.

Successful marketing comes down to this: *Keeping things simple, focused, but consistent. It all has to fit and make sense; it has to be a strategy that is right for you and your business. But you have to be consistent with it.*

You can't market for one day but expect to see the results from marketing for thirty!

Chapter Seven

FROM LEAD TO SALE

ow comes the part that I love the most, the selling. Which if you'd have said that to 18-year-old me or even a 16-year-old me, she would have laughed in your face. I used to despise selling; I used to associate selling with those doorstep sellers and the ones that crowd around you when you step foot into an electrical store.

I also used to have this belief that I can't sell, I was shy and generally not someone who enjoyed socialising and so the idea of selling to people used to fill me with dread. I was sure and adamant I couldn't sell, then I started my first business, and I quickly found out that everything I had ever told myself or believed about selling was totally false.

Selling isn't the bad guy, selling isn't this big bad wolf, like some believe, and I believe anyone can sell!

You may be reading this shaking your heads thinking "no Jane, I absolutely cannot sell", but the truth is you can you just haven't allowed yourself to see it yet but that's where this chapter comes in. If you're looking for sales scripts, you won't find one here, and I'll explain why that is, but by the end of this chapter not only will you believe you can sell, but you'll know how to do it too.

One question I am always asked when it comes to high-end selling is "Do I need to sell differently?" the honest answer is no, selling is the same regardless of the figure, it doesn't matter whether you're selling something that's 1k or 100k selling is the same. But it's interesting how people's thoughts and feelings around high-end and low-end selling can be so different.

So many people and perhaps you reading this right now have this belief that high-end selling is harder than selling something low-end, because the price is more they and perhaps you automatically assume that it's a harder sell, it costs more, therefore, getting the yes must be more difficult. But it isn't, in fact, I used to hold the opposite belief.

I used to believe that selling high-end was easier than selling low-end. Why? Because that's what my experience has led me to believe, that's the belief and story I had created around selling. Give me something 50k to sell, and I can do it click of the finger, but something £500 felt like pulling teeth.

But that's actually one of the foundational points of selling, is what you actually believe about selling in the first place, what we allow ourselves to believe, feel and see about selling has a direct impact on how we sell and whether we actually get the sales we're desiring.

Limit The Worry & Pre-Qualify

I'm sure if you've spent any amount of time in the online world, you'll have come across the words "pre qualifying" most people use pre-qualifying as a way to ensure the only people they're getting on sales calls with are people who are a good fit for what they're selling, but I actually find pre-qualifying can have another purpose and that is how it impacts you.

When we think about why most people are nervous when it comes to sales calls and conversations, it'll usually be linked to the money aspect, the part where they have to ask for the sale, the part where the amount that this cost has to leave their lips and be said out loud.

I can remember the first time I was selling a high-end package for my coaching business on a call, and I sat there almost all through the call thinking to myself "Jane you're going to have to actually say this figure out lout" which is interesting really as I had sold many things before without any issue, but the minute I was essentially selling myself those thoughts crept in, and I'll talk more about that in a minute. We all have them, everyone has them, and usually, the nerves are attached to that asking for the sale part.

Pre-qualifying can help with that; it can act as a sort of placebo effect in many ways. You worry that they won't be able to afford it or you worry about that moment you have to tell them the price well pre-qualifying is a way of in your mind anyway taking the worry of those moments away.

If as part of the pre-qualifying you're asking them to ensure they read your offers or if as part of the pre-qualifying you're asking if they're in a position to purchase now or are they researching etc, you can directly use that to lessen the nerves and that voice.

In our heads if they already know the cost or if you already know their position on purchasing it automatically makes it feel lighter and less of a worry, "they already know" you can tell yourself, and so the big heavy worry and nervous feeling that people have around asking for the sale part can actually be lessened by pre-qualifying.

But pre-qualifying has many other advantages too, it also means you won't be wasting your time, and I mean this in the nicest possible way as I believe that no conversation is a waste of time. Still, some conversations are more valuable than others, and different conversations should be dealt with in different ways. For example, let's say someone isn't a fit to work with you but is a fit to be a referer for you, well instead of wasting their and your own time on a sales call that was never going to be of benefit to them you'd be better off directing them somewhere else, pre-qualifying isn't just about you it's actually about them as well.

Often pre-qualifying is all pointed towards being of benefit to the one selling, but actually, it's just as valuable to the one you're selling to and in fact, can go a long way in building better relationships with those who aren't a fit quite yet.

I've had people who have shown interest in working with me on specific packages but who simply haven't been a fit for them, instead of letting them go down the rabbit hole and go through a sales call or conversation with me and then selling them into something that clearly wasn't a fit I tell them upfront and that has actually gone a long way to benefit me further down the line.

They've appreciated my honesty, and they've appreciated the fact that I haven't wanted to waste their time or sell them into something that isn't a fit for them. Months or even years in some cases later they've come back and bought when they were a fit, but this made them feel as if they also had more confidence and trust in me, so when they were ready and when they did know they were a fit they came straight back.

Had I not pre-qualified them, then I wouldn't have known that it wasn't right for them until we had both used valuable space in our time.

But there is also an element of pre-qualifying that can work against people, in this day and age speed is a key part of purchasing, think about it we've gone from cash, cheques, signing with your card to now being able to pay with your phone, one-click amazon button exists for a reason, and it exists because speed is what the consumer craves but also speed in the sales process reduces the time they have for objections to come in.

Think about your own buying habits, you're in a queue, and you're paying with cash, you have the cash there in your hand, and there is a long queue. You are far more likely to debate whether you actually need or want what you're buying, the queue is long, and you have to physically hand over the cash, a large percentage of people in this scenario won't buy. They won't buy because that objection voice has a chance to really take hold. Change the scenario, there's no queue, and you're using your phone to pay, one tap and you'll have purchased, you're not handing anything over, you're not physically giving the cash, and the queue is non-existent, the time you have to debate is minute, and therefore a much larger percentage will actually purchase.

The danger with pre-qualifying is that some people do it in such a way that draws out the process, that creates more walls, that slows the process down instead of speeding it up and what that results in is people not buying, even though they may have been an ideal client, and even though they may have had the money readily available, they don't convert with you because you don't have the speed element.

This is where with pre-qualifying you need to strike a balance, the balance between pre-qualifying to ensure you have hot leads but not having a pre-qualifying system that draws the whole sales process out to the point where their objections can come in, and that voice can talk them out of going any further.

But you have to get on the phone with everyone to sell high end, so having long questionnaires is necessary as a barrier right?

No, I used to think it was. I used to think that in the online world if you're selling high-end packages, you had to have questionnaire and then if you thought they were ok from the questionnaire you allow them to have a call and then from the call you'd sell and so on, but half the time that made no sense to me!

From my point of view that's drawing a sales process out completely unnecessarily, and I've lost count of the number of people who end up losing leads who don't get emails to say that they've been accepted to book a consultation call etc.

Now I'm not saying that you definitely shouldn't have questionnaires and that you shouldn't vet people, you absolutely can but don't be boxed into thinking it's the only way. I make high-end sales daily straight from my website without speaking to them, they pay in full on my website without booking a call first, and you might be thinking "but don't you end up with people you don't like?" No, I used to think that as well, I used to think that you had to get on the call with them because high-end means you're going to want to make sure they're definitely people you want to work with, but here's the thing, I only call in people I definitely want to work with, my content and marketing only speaks to these people, and so the chances of someone booking one of my high-end packages and not being a good fit for it is almost non-existent.

I have the option of a call should they want one, but I don't make it compulsory. It works for me, and it works for many of my clients, but equally, I have clients who do have a call as a compulsory part of their sales process, it can all work, which is the thing to remember along this journey, you are not in a box with a set of rules to follow, you can make your own rules, create your own box or not have a box at all.

The key with pre-qualifying is to do it without having it compromise on your speed; it should enhance your sales not take away from them, it should add value to your sales process not devalue it.

You can pre-qualify through your marketing and through your content, you can pre-qualify through the copy you use in your sales copy. If you do use the questionnaire route be sure that the system behind it is quick and simple, if it's six days before you get back to them with a calendar link you'll likely have lost them. Ideally it needs to be instant, they fill the form they schedule the call, you can always have a disclaimer to say that the booking is provisional. Either way, don't mistake pre-qualifying for creating loads of hoops for people to jump through just because someone isn't willing to jump through 30 million hoops doesn't mean they weren't going to buy, it just means they were ready to buy right now and not 30 million hoops later when you told them they could!

Conversions start with your beliefs.

It's interesting when I speak to people about high-end selling almost all of their objections as to why they can't do it come from the beliefs in which they hold around high-end selling.

"I can't because I'm not that valuable."

"But don't you need to be able to shower them with things."

"I can't sell at that price."

"It's for people who have been in business longer than me."

It's also always interesting to discover that people who are trying to sell at a higher level currently and getting no sales also have these beliefs, but here's the thing if you don't believe you're valuable then why would anyone else?

If you're making high-end selling this big bad scary wolf, then you're going to struggle to get the sale. Successful selling comes from you, it comes from your energy, and your energy comes from the beliefs that you hold.

I mentioned how I had a belief that high-end selling was easier than low-end selling, well that had a direct impact on the conversions I saw on my low-end items. Just like people who have a belief that high-end selling is more difficult will struggle to sell high end.

The reality is though that there is only one difference between selling anything and that is the price, and the price is just a bunch of numbers. What you make those numbers mean however has a direct result in the sales you make.

If you believe you're not good enough to sell at that number then you won't, if you believe you're not a big enough name or don't have a valuable enough result then again you won't sell at that number.

But the thing is those beliefs, all of them, no matter what they are can be changed. They can be changed into a belief that means you can, one that believes you can and one that means you get those sales.

It's interesting in my first business I never considered that I wasn't valuable enough, I wasn't selling myself as such, I sold my first high-end package after three months in business, and I didn't once consider whether I was valuable enough or not and yet, when it came to selling myself through my coaching a whole world of beliefs around high-end selling came to the surface that I had never even thought of before, but they all had one theme around them, and that was what I was making high-end selling mean.

I believed that I had to be a bigger name. I believed that I had to be more valuable. I believed that I had to ...but the thing is it isn't actually about me. Sure it may feel like I am selling me, but I'm not, I'm selling the result, the outcome, the want and I know for sure they are valuable, they're valuable because of the difference it makes in my ideal clients lives in all different areas, not just money but relationships, health, their life as a whole changes and that is valuable.

When I reframed how I looked at it, when I stopped making it about me and instead made it about the impact, the value, my ideal client, I was able to change my beliefs, and I went from 0 to over 40k in under thirty days, I went on to make 100k in under six months, all high-end sales but none of them would have happened had I not changed my beliefs around high-end selling.

Your sales results start and end with your beliefs, change your beliefs, and you will change the sales results you see in your business, but without doubt, if you don't change your beliefs around high-end selling, you will not sell at that level.

You have to believe in your value; you have not to make high-end selling this big bad wolf, you may have once overheard a conversation that said: "people who charge high prices are money grabbers."

One of my first clients said those exact words to me; she said: "I really do believe my coaching is valuable and I believe in my work, but I read this whole thread in a group where people were saying coaches who charge high prices are money grabbers."

This isn't a one-off either, I see the posts, I roll my eyes, but for others, they take them on board, I also once upon a time used to think I was perhaps doing wrong charging a high-end price, but the thing is there are always people out there in every industry charging various different amounts.

Does it make one more right than the other? No

You can buy a face mask for under $5, but you can also go and have a face mask that will cost you $50k (look it up they do exist) my point is that there's always differently priced services and products in every sector and those beliefs those people hold around money grabbers are precisely that, their own beliefs.

I asked my client if she believed she actually was, aside from this thread did she have any evidence that she was a money grabber and was she doing this just for the money.

She didn't even have to think about it the answer was no, she wasn't, and she didn't have any proof other than this thread.

The reality is she was valuable; you are valuable, and why should other people's beliefs stop you from showing that value to the world and charging your worth?

Charging your worth and high-end selling is not icky, it's not money grabbing not unless you have the belief that says it is, the reality is it isn't.

Think about the value you bring; think about the difference your services and coaching makes, are you valuable? You bet you are and why shouldn't you claim that in the world?

High-end selling enables you to serve and impact at the highest level whilst also impacting and serving yourself, and no I'm not going to hide from that either, your life should also light you up, impact you and enable you to live it in the way you desire and that isn't something you should be ashamed of or shy away from either.

So instead of seeing high-end selling as this icky thing see it as this empowering tool, one which doesn't just change your own life but will have a ripple effect of impact across the world, changing multiple lives and impacting people everywhere as a result.

Instead of seeing high-end selling as this huge number, see it as your value and the value that your ideal clients absolutely believe in and want.

Instead of seeing high-end selling as some parts of the internet would have you believe, see it as how you choose, create your own beliefs, more empowering and impactful ones, beliefs that enable you to step into your true power!

What you do before sales calls has a direct impact on what you'll hear on it.

When most people are thinking of sales calls they're looking for tips and tricks as to what they can say or do on the sales call to get the conversion, but actually what you do before the sales call has the biggest impact.

Let's say you're nervous as hell about sales calls; I can assure you of one thing no matter what you say or do on that call you'll likely still not get the yes. Because your energy is planted firmly in that nervous space, this isn't to say you can magically click your fingers and the nerves go away.

I used to be nervous as hell before sales calls, I'm not ashamed to admit I'd feel sick and all sorts, sweaty palms right up until I got on the call. I'd even sit there sometimes thinking "please don't answer" which is crazy really considering I wanted the sales!

But I know there are many of you who feel the same way, who experience the same feelings and the same voices. The thing is those feelings and voices don't fuel us, and they don't benefit us on sales calls.

There isn't however a magic wand you can wave to get rid of the feeling magically, you can, however, feel nervous without having the nerves impact your energy on the call, in fact, however, you might feel about sales calls, you may lack confidence, you may be unsure if you can sell it's ok to feel like that, but not allowing the energy to control you on the call is the key.

Which is why what you do before the call really matters.

Recently I had a client who had struggled to make sales for months go from no sales to replacing her whole yearly corporate income in just two weeks, and the biggest change she made was what she did before sales calls. So this stuff matters!

I like to call them pre-sales calls rituals, but everyone should have them, I still have them now even though I feel very differently about sales calls I still have some rituals before the call to ensure I am in the best energetic space.

Remember that we require different energies for different tasks and activities, and sales calls are no different. The first thing to do is figure out which energy serves you best on sales calls; it's likely to be based around confident, high vibe, empowering VS nervous, afraid, lacking belief.

Once you know the energy that serves you on the sales call, then it's about creating a pre-sales call ritual that enables you to get into that space.

My ritual when I was really nervous used to be, listening to a high vibe playlist whilst journaling out some affirmations and journaling on "I am…" (I am confident, I am powerful, I make sales with ease…)

Other people get active before a call; they may repeat affirmations in a mirror; one of my clients does EFT before her sales calls, some dance, some read. What you do really does depend on what brings you into a different energetic space, but figure out what that is and then create a ritual before sales calls that enable you to step into that space.

It isn't about never being nervous, it isn't about ever being afraid, but if you go into the call with a different energy, those thoughts won't control the call and certainly won't be the energy that you give off which means you'll be able to approach the call from a higher power space.

What do I say?

You don't say as much as you think you should!

And if you're hoping for a sales script from me you're going to be disappointed; I genuinely hate those things. And no I'm not being dramatic I genuinely hate sales scripts and here's the thing, they don't work!

99% of people know when a sales script is being used, and they will switch off. They will just detach from it because they know a sales script is being used. The secret to selling is to really listen and be guided by the person on the other end, make them feel like a person and not a number and sales scripts don't achieve that.

The thing with sales calls is that it's less about what you say and more about how well you listen, the sales conversion won't be done in what you say but in what you've listened to and where you've taken the conversation after listening.

It is by far one of the biggest mistakes people make on sales calls, they talk and talk and talk, especially when it comes to the offer part. But here's the thing, if you listen more than you talk and if you pay attention by the time the offer part comes around they'll already have sold themselves into it.

Ask, but more importantly listen to what they say, listen to what they're sharing, what they're letting you know and then allow the conversation to be guided from there instead of ok I have these five questions, and I'm going to ask these like some sort of robot.

People want to feel listened to; people want to feel as if you're actually interested and paying attention. To achieve that you need to listen. They will tell you every-thing you need to know to convert them successfully.

But then comes the part where you have to ask for the sale, you have to make the offer and for a lot of people that fills them with dread and what happens if they experience a case of verbal diarrhoea for two main reasons.

1. They get afraid of the silence (they assume it means they'll hear a no)
2. They think to show the value they have to make it look like there's all this stuff in there

That verbal diarrhoea does the opposite of getting the sale, that verbal diarrhoea actually pretty much guaran-tees the sale won't happen. Instead of helping the conversion you slam the door shut and you'll more than likely hear an "I'll need to think about it" response.

Silence isn't a bad thing; in fact, silence is a good thing on sales calls, which goes against almost everything I was ever told during my brief stint working in the call centre. They were all about never let the person think, silence is bad you need to keep talking, but they were wrong, and they're still wrong now.

Silence isn't bad; without silence, the poor person on the

other side has no time to think. Has no time to process any of the information they're being given and so when you're then asking them to make a decision their brain goes BOOM I don't know!

They don't know because they've been bombarded.

They don't know because they've literally been given no time to think.

You may think silence means you'll hear no but silence means they're thinking, they may have a question, they may just be processing it, and you'll hear a yes, but one thing is for sure trying to avoid the silence is going to end up in one thing, and that's a person on the other end who isn't in a position to say yes because they've had no time to think.

You're also not going to show value on a call by throwing everything and the kitchen sink at them, remember when I talked about when creating your high-end package not to throw everything in there as it actually devalues instead of increasing value? Well, it's the same principle here, if you throw everything and the kitchen sink at them you're going to be drowning out the value.

They'll see the value when you allow them to focus on it, when you focus on it and when you repeat the valuable aspects of the offer. When you refer them back to what they told you they wanted (if you listened you'll know this), you'll show value when you pull out the key aspects of the offer and attach it to what they've told you they need and want, that's where you get them into a space where they go YES I need this.

When you're making the offer remember those two key points, if you forget everything else but just remember those two things you will see a difference on your sales calls. Don't assume silence is a bad thing; you have to give people the space to think. And you'll show value by focusing in on the things they see as valuable which is the want.

Do people actually pay in full?

Do they?

Do people possibly pay in full for five-figure or more packages?

You see people online saying they've closed these big figure packages and you might be thinking, where on earth do they find these people who'll pay five figures in full for a package?

They do exist, but I had the same thoughts myself. I had previously sold high figure packages to corporates, but I wasn't convinced that individuals do the same. When I was selling my first 10k package I can remember thinking to myself, would anyone ever pay in full for this?

I was making sales on it but not paid in full ones, and I got lost trying to figure out where I was going wrong.

Then it was pointed out to me that I wasn't even making it an option. That hit me because they were right; I wasn't.

When selling this offer I led with the payment plan, I sort of wiped pay in full off as an option, didn't even make it possible for people and yet I was sitting there wanting them to.

Of course, it isn't necessarily as simple as just asking but it got me thinking, if I wasn't making it an option and I wasn't leading with it then, of course, they wouldn't pay in full.

So I decided to flip it around and make pay in full my default option for everything, but I also decided to add some bonuses in order to pay in full. Nothing dramatic, nothing drastic but enough to be a nice bonus for someone who wanted to pay in full.

The first week I did it I sold every single one of my sales

pay in full, every sale ranging from 3k to 10k all paid in full.

And I literally made two changes, offered a pay in full bonus, but I made payment in full the default, I didn't lead with its X payments of X but led with the investment as its full amount.

None of them asked about my payment plans, none of them even contemplated it.

For some people pay in full isn't something they're bothered about, and that might be you but if you're someone who would love pay in full then just know that it's possible and there are so many people out there willing to pay it. 90% of all my sales are pay in full, I have no issue with payment plans but my personal preferences is payment in full. There isn't a right or wrong, but if you do desire pay in full, then you have to be setting it up so that payment in full can happen.

Nothing can happen if you're not giving it the space for it to happen, you won't make any sales if you don't ask for the sale, you won't celebrate pay in full if you're not giving people the option to pay in full.

If they don't say yes there and then they're not an ideal client

I couldn't disagree more with this statement, and it

really annoys me when I see it plastered around the place. The fact is that there are plenty of people who do need to check something, who do need a day to think about it before they say yes but that doesn't mean they're not an ideal client of yours.

I have a ridiculously high conversion percentage as do my clients, but I don't dismiss those who don't say yes on the call, I don't throw them in a bucket and say they didn't say yes they're not an ideal client because that's simply not the case.

Just because someone wants to discuss it with someone else doesn't mean they're weak or that they're not going to say yes.

In fact, this whole idea that people aren't allowed to go and chat their decision over with others is ludicrous as is the whole pressure selling in general.

Look sales make the business world go around sure they do, but we don't need to be ass holes while doing it and taking time to remember that it's a human you're speaking to and deal with them in a way you'd appreciate yourself goes a long way.

I've had plenty of people who haven't converted on the call come back a week or even a few months later and purchase, and they have been some of my most amazing clients. But I treated them like a human and hey, if people want to say that makes me a failure at selling then so be it but my sales results say different, and I've done it whilst treating people as humans.

Follow-ups, in my opinion, are important and any business expert trying to tell you not to do them or that anyone who doesn't say yes on the call isn't important in my opinion isn't a business expert at all.

Follow-ups are not to be ashamed of, and by not doing them you are leaving sales on the table, that being said follow-ups also need to be done in an effective way and a random message every now and again with "hey want to work with me yet" isn't going to work.

First of all, organising and agreeing on a follow-up whilst on the call is ideally what you want to be organising.

But after that, how do you follow up in a way that means you'll eventually get the conversion when they're ready? You make them feel like a human!

You don't just see following up as popping on their radar every few weeks but rather see it as a way of increasing your relationship with them.

Instead of just sending them a random message put

some thought into it, send them a blog you've seen that you thought would be of interest to them, direct them to a video or something you think would benefit them. Let them feel as if you're thinking of them.

Instead of a message asking them how business is going , send them a message relating to something you've seen them do, say or achieve recently, make them feel as if you're paying attention to them!

The key with following up is to do it in a way that makes them feel as if you're seeing them as a person and are actually paying attention and wanting to help them, vs just randomly popping up in their inbox to ask if they're ready to buy yet!

Chapter Eight

IT'S NOT ENOUGH TO JUST SAY YOU WANT IT

*9*0% of people who say they want it won't ever make it happen, not because they don't want it because I'm sure on some level they do, but because they never fully commit to it.

Whether your goal is to supercharge your results, whether it's to hit your first 10k month, 100k month or 50k week whatever your goal is you're going to have to fully commit to it to make it happen.

I used to think that people who would say "goal setting doesn't work" were a little crazy. I mean sure it works, it works for me all the time.

But it wasn't until I sat down and really started to think about the difference between those who hit their goals and those who don't and then when I started coaching I was able to look at it on an even deeper level.

There's plenty of goals I've set that I haven't hit and for a while, I thought it was just one of those things, you win some you lose some, I hadn't ever considered there was anything bigger at play until I really looked at it and discovered there actually was.

For all the goals I hit, I did something that I didn't do for those that I didn't, and that was I made it completely non-negotiable. There wasn't an if or a but it was completely and utterly 100% non-negotiable.

I had a client who moved abroad this year, it was a big goal of theirs, but when we started working together they were dead against goals, goal setting doesn't work, it never works they'd say. So when it came to their dream of moving abroad, I challenged them on their beliefs around goals, and I had them do something they'd never done before which was set a goal and then make it non-negotiable.

In six weeks they'd made their move abroad happen!

Not only had they hit their goal, something that they'd never done before but they had made more in those six weeks than they'd made in their previous two years of business. What had they actually done?

They followed my non-negotiable goal success formula, stayed committed to it and from that made it happen. When I talk about making something non-negotiable, I'm not just talking of that surface-level stuff, the level where you go "I really want this" sure, I'm sure you do, but you have to make that really want this a non-negotiable on all levels, feel it, believe it, know deep down in your soul it is happening, that's non-negotiable.

People often get frustrated when they get told not to hold on to their goal; it's frustrating because they have this idea of well, if I'm not supposed to hold on to it how will I then take action to make the goal happen if I'm not even thinking about the goal, and they're right, it can seem a little confusing, but that's where making things non-negotiable comes in.

When you make things non-negotiable you don't need to hold onto it, because it is a done deal, it is a done deal on every single layer of the planet and within you. You, therefore, don't need to hold onto it in the same way that people feel they need to do when they just set a goal that they say they want.

Goal setting on its own doesn't work, just saying you want to hit these bigger figures or sell these higher packages on their own doesn't work, but put it all together and tie it with a non-negotiable ribbon, and you've got a package that is the secret to hitting your goals.

But is it even safe for you?

Is it safe for you?

Your goal?

Is it safe for you to reach it?

Is it safe for you to make it happen?

On the surface, the answer to that might be yes sure of course it is, but deep down often something else is at play which means it isn't and if we don't believe something is safe for us we simply won't allow ourselves to make it happen.

When we have a goal, that goal will ultimately lead to a change, whether we see that change as positive or positive or a combination of two largely comes from the beliefs that we hold.

Let's take my client who had a goal of moving abroad as an example, moving abroad was going to open so many doors, it was going to enable them to live a life of freedom that they had been dreaming of, but it also had some beliefs attached to it that made the goal far less safe for them.

"I'll be alone."

"I don't know how to cook I'll starve."

"I won't have my environment as an excuse anymore."

Moving abroad whilst having plenty of positives also had negatives. Those negatives would stop them from making it happen; it wasn't safe; it actually felt really unsafe.

When people set goals they usually focus on the positives, which is absolutely important and I'll get to that in a minute, but you also have to be aware that if you're not aware of any beliefs or stories or feelings that you have that means the goal isn't safe for you, then you're likely not to make the goal happen.

It's about being aware, and that's a large part of growth, making things happen, making goals happen is being aware of what's happening and aware of your thoughts, beliefs, self-sabotaging etc.

You might be thinking no, I don't have anything attached to my goal that makes it not safe for me, but it could be the simplest of things. Reaching the goal you desire right now may change things for you, maybe it would change how much attention you get and then suddenly that voice of "omg we can't be seen like that" comes in.

Sometimes it's the smallest of things, I've worked with clients who had this belief that it wasn't safe for them to reach that goal because then they'd be seen and the parents at the school gates would suddenly know what they did and would take the piss out of them.

Hell, I've had it myself just whilst writing this book, the goal of publishing a book didn't feel safe for me to begin with either due to those underlying beliefs I had and yet here I am!

Having underlying beliefs making a goal not safe for you isn't something to be ashamed of, but neither is it something you should ignore or just push under the carpet and pretend doesn't exist, because it's that voice, those beliefs that are going to hold you back from making your goals non-negotiable and in the end hold you back from reaching the goals and the very life that you desire.

You may feel it isn't safe for you because you have some underlying beliefs about high-end selling mean more responsibility or that level of selling means more pressure.

It could be anything, and it could just as easily be nothing, but you have to explore it so you can become aware, so you can change, deal with and confront those beliefs enabling you to then move forward making a goal non-negotiable whilst being completely prepared and putting yourself in a space where you can make these goals happen.

The first thing to do is explore what changes for you once you hit this goal. What changes when you hit 10k weeks, 10k months, sell high-end, hit 200k months, sell out of your high-end packages?

What changes happen in all areas of your life, not just "I'll have more money" but what does the money mean, what do the sales mean will happen? (that you believe)

Do relationships change?

Does how you behave change?

Does how others view you change?

Will more people know about you?

Explore every area and angle of your goal, become completely and utterly aware of every negative belief you have attached to your goal that is currently on some level going to make the goal non-negotiable for you and then deal with it!

Create and install new beliefs; remind yourself why these beliefs aren't true. Just because your belief says that everyone at the school gates would be laughing at you is that true, what proof do you have of that and does it even matter to you that much if they do?

Then focus on why the goal is safe for you, make it safe for you. Install those beliefs about the positive changes, remind yourself and your subconscious why this goal isn't just safe for you but why you want to reach it.

If it doesn't mean anything, it'll just be empty words.

Your goals have to mean something to you; there's no getting around it if your goals aren't yours and if they don't mean anything to you then making it non-negotiable is going to be impossible.

I can remember setting goals that weren't mine; I thought they were goals people were supposed to have, those ones society tells you that you should have, those ones that would impress people even.

Equally never apologise for your goals, they are yours, and you should own them, not apologise for them. I see people apologising for their goals being too big, or for wanting too much or for whatever other reason.

Whether your goals are big, small or anything in

between doesn't and shouldn't matter to anyone other than you, and apologising for them is something you should never do. They are yours, they should mean something to you, and if others have a problem with it, that's on them and their own set of beliefs.

You shouldn't dim your goals to pacify others, but likewise, you shouldn't enlarge your goals to impress people either.

If you don't want the yacht doesn't set it as a goal, if you want to live in a small house in the middle of nowhere with no tv and just books then do that, if it's what lights you up then do that.

Which is where knowing your why of your goal comes in, your goal should spark, inspire and motivate you; it should light a fire inside of you that when you think of it warms you up with joy and excitement, anything less and you should forget it!

But connecting to your goal isn't just about going "My goal is to make XYZ" your why is behind that, your why is why you want to make that amount, what's behind it, what changes not just for you but for your life as a whole, including those you serve?

How does the goal impact you?

Impact your life?

Others around you?

Those you work with?

The world as a whole?

That's where you discover your goal while so many people set surface level goals that they're not even really connected to and they'll spend their whole lives trying to reach a goal that they didn't even really want or understand.

But you're here to live limitlessly, so what does that even look like? How does that goal help you do that? How does that goal feel in your life, and what do you see as a result of reaching that goal?

That's your why, that's the goal that you want to focus on, not the figure, not the amount, not the thing but the why.

We're more likely to reach something we feel emotionally attached to than something we feel distant and not connected to.

Throw that anchor down

When someone first said to me about anchoring my goal, I was a little "what the hell do they mean?" I've set a goal; I'm connected to it what on earth is anchoring it in.

But then the more I thought about it, the more I realised that was something I had always done, for every goal I had ever hit I had always anchored the goal in.

It's part of making those goals non-negotiable for me, being in the space where the goal is anchored in on every level, that's where the being able to let it go and have full trust in the goal happening comes from.

It comes from the goal being anchored into every single part of you.

It comes from feeling the goal, from being able to close your eyes and energetically being there in that space and feeling as if the goal is your reality right now, that's where it's a done deal, that's where the done deal energy comes from.

But how do you do it?

Do you just sit there, visualise and then bang it's anchored in?

Well, I actually think how you do it depends on you, what works for some doesn't work for others. It could be that visualising it does enable you to anchor it in. I have clients who record themselves being in the space where the goal has happened, and they listen to that twice a day, I have clients who'll journal and tap on it. I also have clients who just remind themselves daily it's a done deal and visualise complete with smells etc.

One way I love is to incorporate it into something I already do daily which is my gratitude journaling, so as well as being grateful for what I already have I include being grateful for the goals that I am currently aiming for, being grateful from the space of it being a done deal.

I also like to really step into the space where I can anchor it in down to how my surroundings would feel, look and smell.

With my client who desired to move abroad part of the anchoring in was them visualising the sea breeze, the smell of the air, the feeling of sand in between their toes.

For some people visualising simply doesn't work, and writing has more power, for others, writing holds no power, but audio does. The point is to find a way that works for you, it could be a combination of all of it or just one thing, but don't just write a goal, visualise it and anchor that goal in so it's in the space where you feel beyond doubt it is happening.

Accountability holds power

I think accountability is way more powerful than most people actually give credit for, but equally, if you're setting the accountability without everything else around it then it doesn't work, and you actually end up moving into a space where you worry and feel afraid with the goal as now you've gone and made yourself accountable and you're not going to make it happen, and it snowballs from there.

In that sense and in that space, accountability doesn't work, but when it's done combined with everything else, accountability has added power.

We are always more likely to make something happen once we've said it out loud, once we've put ourselves in a space where we are accountable. Mainly because we don't want to be the person who doesn't do it, we don't want to have to explain why it didn't happen or work or anything else. So from a motivation place, we will use accountability to be that rocket under our asses shall we say.

But it has to be part of the whole picture and not just accountability on its own; otherwise, it doesn't act as that rocket and instead acts more like a bomb sitting in your pocket that you wait to go off and then have to pick up the pieces afterwards.

Accountability in the right way is positive but in the wrong way can actually paralyse us and paralysing us isn't a good way to reach our goals.

But what are we actually talking about when it comes to accountability?

Well much like everything else I think this comes down to yourself, for some people going and telling the world works, for others, private accountability can work just as well. I tend to find myself a combination of the two works.

I'll take my book as an example, as it's a bigger thing I actually used both private and public. I told the world I was releasing a book and when, I also in private did the same that then gave me accountability from all angles, something which worked as you're now reading the book and it was released on time!

Sometimes I'll just use my private circle and have them keep me accountable but other times letting the wider world play a part works for me. However, you need to understand and be aware of yourself.

I know for some people going and telling the world wouldn't actually hold the same power that it does perhaps for me, it would cause them to paralyse, be completely consumed by fear and worry and then wouldn't take the steps forward. That accountability isn't positive; it's negative and one you want to avoid.

Equally, be honest with yourself as to why it may not have worked in the past or why you're worried about letting the world keep you accountable, is it really because it isn't something that would work for you or is it more your fear voice not wanting you to? Because there is a difference.

Asking people in your private circle to keep you accountable is good, but equally, you'll want to set out some clear rules, those in our private circle are likely to be a little wary of how far they push you or not wanting to feel like they're bothering you, and so the accountability whilst on paper may exist in reality it doesn't.

The solution? Be clear with them about what you'd like them to do and give them permission to remind you that you asked for it, screenshot the message for example. You have to remember that if you're asking them to keep you accountable and support you by checking in or mentioning it or keeping you to a timescale that you're giving them permission to kick your ass, and so you can't then go and blow up at them when they do that, which you may not think you would, but trust me we've all been there, and the reality is that it can and does happen.

Don't just set it, make it non-negotiable.

Making your goal non-negotiable is about using all the above but also adding one ingredient into it. Taking some sort of action, doing something that takes the goal from being something you "could" make happen to something that absolutely is happening.

I do this every time I set a goal, and without fail, it doesn't let me down, the times I don't do it is when the goal doesn't happen.

My client who had a goal of moving abroad also swears this was the secret ingredient for them.

In their case making it non-negotiable was booking their one-way flight, it terrified them to do it, but it was also the very thing they needed to do.

Booking the one-way flight ticket meant they went from, "I would like to move abroad" to "I am moving abroad", it completely shifted their energy and that combined with everything above meant the goal was non-negotiable.

It wasn't an if, or a maybe or an I could, it was a complete and utter done deal.

The ticket was booked, they were going.

It's actually funny because now almost 12 months later when we were chatting about them making this goal happen, they said they just never doubted it, they never doubted that they were going to make it happen, it was as if they had completely shifted as a person just by setting a goal as non-negotiable.

Something they had never done before, and it's actually something most people don't do. They set a goal and go through the motions but never make it non-negotiable, never put themselves into the space where this goal is 100% happening, no ifs or buts no maybes or clouds, it is happening, and they don't doubt it.

It's a powerful space; it's a space where the magic happens if you will, it's the space that I swear by when it comes to goal setting.

You might be thinking what on earth could you do for this final step to make your goal non-negotiable, for some it might be a big thing like booking that one-way flight, but for others, it might be clearing space in your calendar for the high-end clients to come in.

Which you may think sounds really small but the reality is for most people who set goals they're not creating a space where the goal can even happen, let's say you want to sign five high-end clients, but you have no space in your calendar, then where would they go?

Clearing the space in your calendar and even booking some high-end work in makes a big difference, you are then saying to the universe and the world that you are ready, and this is happening.

So making it completely non-negotiable doesn't always have to be this huge thing, but take some sort of action and do something that cements that goal completely in as being 100% a done deal in every single part of you and the world!

Chapter Nine

YOU ARE ALWAYS THE KEY TO SUPERCHARGING YOUR BUSINESS & LIFE

*2*0% strategy, 80% mindset you've probably heard that saying a few times before, but it's true. It seems a little crazy, I mean can you have that much of an influence over your results, are you really the key?

Yes is the answer, people spend their lives searching for the magic strategy or the missing piece when in reality they had what they were looking for all along, all they had to do was release it.

When it comes to high-end selling and reaching your sales goals, more often than not something that most people say is "but where will I find people who will pay these prices" or "How will I make this money?" when in reality they are asking the wrong questions.

It isn't about where you'll find them.

It isn't about how you'll make money.

It is about you.

All of it is always about you.

Who you are.

How you think.

How you feel.

What beliefs and stories you hold.

The energy in which you operate from.

How you see your role in making money.

The reality is you never actually make the money, whatever the figure the money already exists in the world. Whether it's 1k, 10k, 100k or more, the money already exists. You don't have to make it. It is already in existence in this world; it exists in bank accounts, cards, stocks and shares and through various other means.

You don't ever make the money, you receive it, you call it in and to do that the question isn't how you do it but rather who you need to be to do it.

Much like where you'll find people who are willing to pay your prices, there are people everywhere; you're surrounded by them, you probably speak to many on a daily basis, they don't walk around with a sign on their head that says "I can afford it" and neither do they all hang out in some secret place. The reality is that they're all around you, the world is full of them, there are people who can pay your prices in abundance the question actually is who do you need to be to attract them?

The version of you right now, who you are at this moment in time probably isn't the version of you who sells high end effortlessly, who supercharges their results and who's living limitlessly. If you were, you'd already be there doing it all. And that's not to say you never can; it's not to say you've been doing anything wrong, it's just you haven't stepped into the version of you who's there yet.

People underestimate how powerful we are, but when you think about it, logically it actually makes sense. Logically all our actions and activities that we do, and what we say, how we say it, comes from ourselves. It comes from our energy, from our thoughts and beliefs, our own mindset.

It's the classic example of you can have two people side by side; they sell the same things; they have the same strategy, one skyrockets the other stays exactly where they are. Why?

Well, ultimately, there is only one difference, and that is the person taking action.

When we're taking action from a place where we're not expecting to make sales, we won't make them, when we're taking action from a place where we feel as if we're not good enough we won't make progress.

Everything, all of it comes from us!

Your Habits Fuel & De-Fuel You

Habits are what we live by, we spend most of our lives operating with habits, our day, week and month is full of them, and yet it's surprising how very little attention we actually pay to them, or most people pay to them anyway.

But habits can make the difference between us reaching our goals and making all of this happen VS not.

The other level of habits is there may be some habits that are perfectly fine for us on the level we currently are, but for the level we desire to get to, the version of you who has supercharged their success, who's selling high-end and living their limitless life, well, they may be living by very different habits.

I used to have a habit of watching TV in bed before

sleep, I knew it wasn't a great habit, but I had thought nothing of it until I was asked the question of what habits the version of me who's reaching the success I was desiring would be living by.

And suddenly I realised that a lot of the habits I currently had, including watching tv in bed before sleep were habits that would not fuel that version of me. So the cull of habits began.

Most people make the mistake of thinking they don't need to make changes until they are actually there, until they have made it happen. When I reach XYZ, I'll stop XYZ.

The reality is though to get to XYZ you have to stop XYZ now. You won't get there if you hold on to and keep the same habits that you wouldn't have if you were already there.

Being honest about the habits that fuel you and don't isn't easy and it isn't easy to stop doing them either, but if you're seriously committed to making your success happen, then it's a challenge you will accept for yourself.

Take a look at your habits, which ones wouldn't fuel you if you were already where you desired to be, if you were already that version of you which habits would you absolutely not have that you currently have now?

Of course, once you've recognised which habits don't fuel you, then you have to think about new habits.

I knew that watching tv in bed before sleep wouldn't be a habit I'd have, it didn't fuel me, and it certainly didn't set me up in a way that would mean the next day I'd be starting it fresh like the version of me who was already at the level I was aiming to get to would.

But what would? What habit would I have that I don't currently have?

For me, it was a simple night routine which involved switching off from technology at least an hour before going to sleep and doing gratitudes as the last thing before I slept.

Water was also another habit that I knew that version of me would be committed to, staying hydrated with water was always an I'll do it when I have a spare five minutes sort of thing, when really that version of me would be hydrated and so having a habit of drinking water instead of waiting until I was thirsty was another positive habit I brought in.

Exercising is usually a classic for people, I'll work out when ...but when never happens right? You workout now to get to that version of you and not wait until you're that version to work out.

Habits can make or break your success, if we're operating from a space that is fuelled by habits that don't actually fuel us we are highly unlikely to be taking action from the space that would enable us to reach our goals.

They may seem really small, but habits are powerful. Having the right ones will fuel you, but having the wrong ones will keep you spinning your wheels and not achieving your goals..

The Space In Which We Work From

Imagine trying to create from a dark, smelly, cramped space, would you achieve much? Would you feel inspired?

The answer is probably not and yet every single day, right across the globe people are doing just that whilst not even really knowing it.

The environment that we work from isn't just about looking at the physical environment but the inner environment as well.

Your environment on all levels and layers has to fuel you, that's what a productive environment is all about.

I used to think of my environment as just being the

physical outer space in which I worked, I actually had that as an excuse for ages, "I'll feel more creative when I move."

The thing was to reach my goal of moving I needed to be working from a better environment, and sure, I didn't feel inspired with the exact physical environment location, but that doesn't mean I couldn't change it. The reality is I could, and I did, if I hadn't, I wouldn't be writing this today having achieved my goal of moving abroad.

Yes, the physical space in which you're working is important, it forms part of your environment and whilst you may not be able to make any big changes to it you can certainly make smaller ones.

The key is to once again connect into the version of you who is already where you desire to be, what's her environment, what does it look and feel like?

Then you bring that into existence right now, if your environment would feel more creative, how can you bring more creative energy into your space right now?

If your environment would feel lighter, how can you bring that energy into your space right now?

But I also said that your environment isn't just about

your outer environment and it isn't, your environment also includes your inner, the inner space where you create and work from which is of course yourself.

I mentioned my habit of not drinking water above, and that actually became part of my environment, the version of me who was already where she desired to be would be hydrated and energised, part of that was ensuring I was fuelled both with fluids and food.

Whilst the outer space in which you're creating from has an impact on your work so does what's going on inside, if you're not fuelled you're not going to be creating from a space or taking action from a space which is fuelled either.

It's like asking a car to drive 500 miles at full throttle when it doesn't have enough fuel onboard to allow it to do that.

If you're not fuelled, if your environment isn't fuelled, then neither will your goals be.

The version of me who was already where I desired to be would feel and be operating from a space that was more energised, whilst being hydrated and fuelled by eating better foods was part of that, I realised that fresh air also helped me have that same energised feeling, and so a daily non-negotiable was then to get outside.

Again connecting to the version of you who is already where you desire to be, how are they fuelled? Are they energised? Are they hydrated? How can you bring that into your environment now?

Self-Care Isn't Selfish.

I say that as a reminder to myself sometimes and actually it's a reminder to me as to how far I've come. In my first business, self-care was non-existent, and I almost repeated that same mistake.

Self-care to me was something that you did when you had time, a luxury so to speak but actually, self-care is the opposite. Self-care is a strategy and a tool that enables you to reach your goals, it isn't wasting time; it's doing something incredibly valuable with your time.

Just like your environment being fuelled, if you're not being refuelled, you will burn out, and not only that but your whole activity, creativity etc. will all suffer as a result.

Self-care became and is now a non-negotiable for me; it doesn't sit at the bottom of the pile but rather the top, instead of viewing it as something that took me away from the business I view it as something that enables me to be in the space where I can grow my business.

It's interesting really almost everyone when picturing the version of themselves who is already where they desire to be almost everyone says that they'd be less busy and practice more self-care, two things that everyone can and should be doing right now to enable them to get there.

Yet most look at free time and self-care as a luxury, a luxury only afforded to those who've "made it" pretty interesting really that as a society we've created that story en masse, and people absorb it, and it's a story they hear right through their life.

Self-care is a luxury.

Only successful people who've hustled every day can have free time.

Everyone is busy.

The fact is that none of that is true, busy is a badge of honour that too many carry, including myself. Oh, successful people are busy, people who work are busy and here's a crazy thing I once thought I had to be busy for people to think I was working!

People I was surrounded by who worked in jobs would always be busy, and so I had this belief that I had to be busy and run ragged like them so they'd think I was working!

Crazy really when I think about it, but I also know that so many others have these same beliefs and these beliefs have us believing that self-care is a luxury, something you only do as a reward or that odd occasion where you have spare time. In reality, it's completely the opposite, and as a society, if we adopted that different belief, we'd see a much happier and more productive world.

You may be one of those who think that self-care is a luxury, but is it really?

Because self-care isn't just going and getting your nails done, self-care is also sitting in a quiet corner reading a book for 30 minutes a day. Self-care can also be taking 15 minutes to listen to some music.

Self-care isn't really about pampering but rather helping you stay in a space where you perform best, helping you stay in a space where you feel so much better, a space where you have time to breathe and think and can operate at a level that you simply cannot operate at if you're not taking that time for self-care in your life.

It doesn't have to take you hours every day; you could take 3 x 30 minutes slots in your day and enjoy some self-care, 90 minutes out of your day that you would otherwise have spent scrolling through social media and it would make a huge difference in your life.

Think for a second back to that version of you that's already where you desire to be, would she be leaving self-care to those rare moments in a year where she has given herself some free time? Or would self-care and refuelling herself be a non-negotiable?

We Are What We Believe

I used to think those people who'd say "we get what we expect" were a little crazy I mean some people expect to win the lottery, and they don't, but then actually that isn't the case. Most people don't expect to win the lottery, they say they'd like to, but they certainly don't expect it.

But if we look at peoples sales results, them reaching their goals, those who "make it" and those who don't they largely do get what they expect, and they do achieve what they believe.

If you go into a sales, call expecting not to make a sale you're almost guaranteed not to.

If you expect only to attract people who won't pay your

prices, that's almost guaranteed that that's who you will attract in.

If you believe you're not good enough, then you won't be.

Because our beliefs and stories, our mindset has a direct effect on how we show up, what we do, how we do it and the energy in which we're doing it with.

In fact, it's crazy to think that one simple change of belief can change your world, but it's true, and it seems really ridiculous and cheesy when you say it or read it, but it really is true.

You only ever need one person to change your life, and that's you, and for a lot of people, they only need to change their beliefs to do it. We pick up so many beliefs; our mindset is influenced by the very youngest moments of our lives, we pick up stories that we carry around with us for years.

Conversations we overheard between family members growing up.

Comments the teachers made at you during your troubled teens.

Throwaway comments that friends had made when you mentioned your goals.

Arguments your parents had that they thought you weren't paying attention to.

It all gets absorbed and some of it we end up carrying around with us in a way that we had never even considered and then suddenly when we are aiming to get to a new level, reach a goal or change our life we see these beliefs, stories and our own mindset in a way we simply didn't before.

That throwaway comment about "money being evil" matters, as it's not a throwaway comment that you've simply remembered anymore but a comment that you took on as a belief, a belief that has held you back from making the money you desire because you don't want people to think you're evil.

I could write a whole book on un-doing and re-learning about yourself and the world; I literally picked up a whole book of limiting beliefs and stories from my childhood and hometown. And I had never really thought any of it mattered until I was growing, until I was getting to those next levels, until I really thought about who I'd be if I was already at those levels, what I'd think, see and believe.

That version of me wouldn't think that rich people were all ass holes, for example (and yes that's a legit belief I held from many conversations I'd overheard). That version of me would believe that money was good; that version of me would be almost the opposite to every belief I had ever held.

I'll be honest; I felt like I was re-doing myself and my mindset completely, un-learning and removing myself from every ridiculous thing I had ever heard and then made my truth.

I bet if you take a second to think about the version of you who's already where you desire to be she'd hold different beliefs to those you hold currently, and I'm sure she'd have a different mindset.

What would you believe?

What stories would you not have anymore?

What would your mindset be?

You may not be convinced; there's a good chance you're reading this thinking what a load of twaddle, my results have nothing to do with what I achieve or get.

I'll say this, I used to be you, and I was wrong, I had a belief that all of this stuff was make-believe but guess where that belief came from, yep it came from jokes and conversations that those from my hometown who were let's say closed-minded about the growth world, coaches, mindset, beliefs etc

But that's why they're still where they are, and I'm where I am!

Don't wait till the end to reward yourself.

It's a curious thing how adults see rewarding; we'll reward kids for doing the small things. Encourage them along and make them feel as if they're doing well and making progress and yet when it comes to ourselves we tend to overlook it and focus on how far we've still got to go.

Yes, I may have achieved that, but I still have ALL of this to do.

Does it really fuel us?

Does the constant idea of having more to do without recognising what we've done really fuel us?

I don't believe it does, in fact, for some people it can have the total opposite effect of fueling. It can make them feel as if they're moving nowhere, doing nothing, miles away from their goals, it can make them feel as if they're never going to make it. And yet if they took a few minutes, they'd actually see they have made progress, is the only progress that matters the big stuff?

I believe in rewarding ourselves, for every part of our journey, including just staying consistent with things, why? Because staying consistent isn't easy and if we're staying consistent but not recognising it and only focusing on the big wins or big sales then we're going to burnout, and we're also going to lose motivation.

By rewarding and recognising the small things, you're not saying that none of the big stuff matters, what you're saying is I matter and my whole journey matters, not just the big things I achieve, you recognise that to get to those bigger goals is a journey and it's a journey made up of small, medium and big things each one a new stepping stone on that journey.

The small consistent steps open doors to the medium ones, and the medium ones make way for the big doors to open and big goals to happen. But none of it happens without the consistent steps; you don't super-charge and jump from 0 to 100 with nothing in between. Supercharging isn't missing everything in the middle; supercharging is staying consistent with the whole journey.

I also think people underestimate just how difficult it is to be consistent with your growth, stepping into the version of you who's already there and battling your fear is tough, being consistent with your activities and habits is tough, so why wouldn't you recognise and reward that?

I'm not suggesting you throw a party every time you stay consistent with something or have a small win, but you should reward yourself. You should take time to recognise your achievements that week, the steps you've taken, the things you've stayed consistent with, they're all wins, they're all going to come together and help you reach those big goals. So reward yourself, recognise all your wins!

Self-sabotage is a bitch, but it happens.

There's no point pretending, self-sabotage is absolutely a bitch but it also happens, it happens to everybody and the idea that it doesn't or won't happen to you isn't going to benefit you.

What will benefit you is being aware of your self-sabotage, understanding what it is, how it works, what triggers it and the signs to look out for.

Self-sabotage is something everybody experiences, whether you've achieved, whether you're halfway up the mountain or at the bottom just starting your journey self-sabotage exists.

It isn't that it stops, it magically disappears when you

reach certain levels, it's more the case that you just get better at dealing with it. You become more self-aware, and unlike previously you don't allow it to take hold and take you down, you don't sit with it, you're aware of it, and you move forward despite its presence.

Self-sabotage is there to pull us back to the levels and comforts where we feel safe and comfortable, it's fear doing its job, and it's mighty good at it too. But getting annoyed it at or seeing it as some sort of enemy won't benefit you.

I see so many people who get annoyed with themselves like they're some sort of failure because they're struggling with it again and I think to myself, but we all experience it.

Because its job is to bring us back to the levels where we feel safe and so if we're aiming to get to a new level of self-sabotage will always come into play, it's always going to try and bring us back because that is what it is designed to do. We're not failures for being human; we just have to find our way of dealing with it, so it doesn't get its wish and hold us back.

Being aware of it isn't easy, and it does take an insane level of self-awareness, but it is possible, it all does, however, start with you being aware of the self-sabotage.

What is it there for?

What usually triggers your self-sabotage?

Once you're aware of it, you can then look at ways in which you can help yourself become aware of when self-sabotage may be triggered for you and indeed if it has been triggered how you can bring yourself back on track.

What this looks like does largely again come down to the individual, what works for some doesn't for others, but having someone on the outside when it comes to self-sabotage can help massively. They are far more likely to be able to see self-sabotage in you VS you see it yourself, particularly to begin with.

Chapter Ten

WHAT COULD IT LOOK LIKE

*Y*ou may be sitting there having read this thinking, it sounds good, I'd love to super-charge my sales through high-end selling, or maybe you love the idea of being able to create a limitless life through high-end selling, but perhaps you're still unsure on what a high-end package could look like for you.

If that's the case, maybe this can be of some inspiration for you. Multiple ideas and examples on high-end packages for various different industries, everything from virtual assistants to hairdressers!

The Fitness Coach

Let's take that the big result of your ideal client right now was to lose 50lbs and by doing that they'll improve not only their health but also their self-confidence, and that will have an impact on their relationships and even their own success.

How could you package a high-end package?

You could take a combination of in-person work (5 days live Bootcamp) and online work (weekly accountability, daily online fitness classes and online nutrition work). That's your initial package, what can you add in to enhance the experience? Bring in a guest to enhance the package, after they've reached their 50lbs weight loss (by thy the end of your package) they get a day personal styling shopping experience so they can dress their new shape and have a wardrobe to match their newfound confidence.

The Virtual Assistant

The big mistake that people make with virtual assistants is assuming it's all just admin work, and if you look at the tasks that virtual assistants do then yes most would just be admin work but if you take the tasks and instead flip it around and sell a specific package towards a specific thing then instantly it's viewed differently.

 Let's say that the ideal client was a coach launching her first online course; she knows the content of the course and how to deliver it but gets completely overwhelmed with everything else.

How could you create a high-end offer?

Intensive (either in person or online) One day to map out a complete online course system, everything from the pre-launch, launch to the delivery of it. All admin and technical stuff. Then there's also the add on sale of having it done for them as well. How could you enhance the experience for them? They could have added support for two months whilst they implement the map you'll have created together on the intensive day itself.

The Hairdresser

You may be thinking there's no way this can work, and if you think of a hairdresser in the traditional sense of the word then probably not no, but if we take the hairdresser and combine it with a valuable package aimed at a specific issue or desire an ideal client will have then, we can make it work.

Let's imagine the ideal client is someone who has been bleaching their hair for quite a long time, it is like straw these days, it's fragile, they can't do anything with it, and they've had enough. But shaving it all off isn't an option for them. They dream of glossy locks.

The offer

Intensive 6-month hair repair and renew treatment plan. Over the course of 6 months, they receive regular treatment and help to repair and renew their hair condition. How could you enhance the experience? Include something bigger that they can have at the end of the six months, something that will help them celebrate having their dream head of hair.

The Life Coach

Life coaches cover a broad spectrum but let's say this life coach specialising in working with mothers, in particular, mothers who have lost themselves after having children and feel constantly drained, overwhelmed and frazzled.

What could the offer look like?

Well the options here are endless (as they are with every sector really), but you could create a 90-day signature package, the end result is a mother who has re-discovered themselves and replaced frazzled with energised. She is happier, and so are her children: fortnightly calls, regular check-ins, and online support. The enhancing the experience could be monthly re-energise hampers which include a variety of items.

The Book Coach

This is a field which is exploding and way more valuable than a lot might think, let's imagine the ideal client is someone who is wanting to write a book but has no idea where to start and who struggles with the confidence that they can write.

The offer

An 8-week package which includes a group 2 or 3-day retreat. They leave the retreat and eight-week package having mapped out their book and have the confidence to write it. Enhance the experience by giving them access to a course on how they would market the book once written and have an upsell of publishing the book for them.

Blogging Expert

I'll be honest, I'm not entirely sure of their official title some call themselves coaches others strategist, but essentially people who help people set up blogs we'll just go with that. The ideal client is someone who currently has a blog but isn't getting traffic and is not making money from it in any way at all.

The high-end offer

A 12-month money-making blog package, the idea is

simple you give them whatever they need during the 12 months so that at the end of the 12 months they have a blog that makes money. How could you enhance it? Perhaps provide them with access to another expert or online courses such as photography (if they need to take better pictures for example)

A small disclaimer I'm not a blogging expert or hairdresser, my field isn't in any of those above so the packages and the contents are simple examples of how a high-end package can be put together for any field.

The message I really want to be able to leave you with after reading this book is that this is possible for anyone and everyone. Even if you're someone who's reading this currently and struggling to sell a one-off hour at $50 or even a small package, don't let your current results hold you back from high-end selling.

High-end selling can supercharge your business, your sales and your life. High-end selling can and will unlock the doors to your limitless living, sometimes it requires you to think outside of the box, sometimes it requires you to jump and do it, but it will always require you to say yes to yourself and your dreams and take action towards them!

If you're ready to start selling high-end.

If you're ready to start selling high-end, supercharge your sales and start living that limitless life you dream of then I'd be more than honoured to help you do it.

Depending on where you are right now and what it is that you're looking for will depend on what's the best next step for you. I don't do cookie-cutter and so helping you find out what's best for you doesn't look like a cookie-cutter approach either. That being said, here are three main ways you can get started!

The High End Online

Are you more of a do it yourself at your own pace type of person? If so, the high end online course is likely a good fit for you; it is designed for the service-based business owner or coach who wants to be selling high end.

Through the course, you'll uncover your high-end message, put your first high-end package together and create an initial plan on how to sell it.

It's do it yourself at your own pace; you can do it all in one week or take nine months it is entirely up to you. Whilst it doesn't come with any support from me, you do get access to some pre-recorded Q&A that cover a wide range of questions to help guide you through the course.

Sound like your type of thing? You can find out more by visiting:

www.janebakercoach.com/highendonline

Free 10k Month Roadmap & Checklist

Do you desire to hit 10k months in your business? For most people that is their starting point, it feels like the first big figure and the big moment in their business. If that's you, then my free download is exactly what you're looking for.

The roadmap & checklist helps you map out what your 10k months look like and how to make them happen for you!

Download your free copy by visiting:

https://www.subscribepage.com/10kmonthroadmap

Unleash Your Limitless Living

My signature 6-month package for service-based business owners and coaches that are ready to sell high end on repeat and claim their limitless life. Whether you're looking to hit 10k months, 100k months or even more this is a package for you.

Not only do we put together a series of high-end packages that are going to have your ideal clients drooling at the prospect of signing up for but we also ensure you have the full package, not just one part of the puzzle but all of it. Not, making sales but hating your life, not feeling free, but no sales. This is about creating a business that makes high-end sales on repeat whilst you live a life without limits that you truly love.

You can find out more by visiting:

www.janebakercoach.com/Unleashyourlimitless

Want to hang out with me some more?

Thank you for purchasing and reading this book, I had so much fun putting it together, and I hope you've enjoyed reading it as much as I did writing it.

But why should the fun end here?

It doesn't have to! Whether you think you'd like to work with me or not, I'd still love to have you join my free community.

I spend a lot of my time there; I love hanging out with the members, and more importantly, I love helping them in the community.

But this isn't just your average community; I don't just open the doors and leave everyone to it. As a member of the free community you'll get access to:

- My monthly free trainings (recent free trainings include How I went from 0 to 40k in under 30 days, How to go from 0 to in demand in under 60 days and How to create a marketing strategy that works)
- Guest expert trainings that happen multiple times each year
- Monthly free 60-minute group coaching call (you vote on the topic, and I'll have open coaching for 60 minutes where I help as many as I can)

And yes it's all free, it doesn't cost you a penny to come in, and I don't have a ton of rules in there either!

You can join at:

www.facebook.com/groups/limitlesslivingwithjane

Printed in Great Britain
by Amazon

22638024R00096